Also by Judith Jones

The Pleasures of Cooking for One
The Tenth Muse: My Life in Food

*With Evan Jones*

The Book of *New* New England Cookery
The Book of Bread
Knead It, Punch It, Bake It!

*With Angus Cameron*

The L.L. Bean Game and Fish Cookbook

# Love Me, Feed Me

# Love Me, Feed Me

## Sharing with Your Dog the Everyday Good Food You Cook and Enjoy

## Judith Jones

Photographs by Chris Vandercook

Alfred A. Knopf   New York   2014

THIS IS A BORZOI BOOK
PUBLISHED BY ALFRED A. KNOPF

www.aaknopf.com

Knopf, Borzoi Books, and the colophon are registered trademarks
of Random House LLC.

Library of Congress Cataloging-in-Publication Data
Jones, Judith, [date]
Love me, feed me : sharing with your dog the everyday good food you
cook and enjoy / Judith Jones.
        pages   cm
        "Borzoi Books."
        Includes index.
    ISBN 978-0-385-35214-7 (hardcover);
    ISBN 978-0-385-35215-4 (eBook)
    1. Dogs—Food—Recipes.   I.  Title.
    SF427.4.J66 2014    636.7'0852—dc23    2014004747

Photograph of M. F .K. Fisher, copyright © Annie Leibovitz/Contact
Press Images, courtesy of Judith Jones: page 149 · Photographs by
Chris Vandercook: pages ii, 7, 8, 10, 12, 25, 33, 39, 41, 42, 45, 47,
54, 57, 60, 61, 63, 69, 74, 77, 85, 95, 110, 117, 125, 132, 141, 150,
152, 178 · Photographs courtesy of Judith Jones: pages 14, 15, 17,
18, 19, 20, 21, 24, 31, 49, 64, 79, 83, 87, 102, 106, 112, 121,
122, 133, 135, 136, 137, 148, 157, 158, 161, 162, 164

Jacket photograph © Chris Vandercook
Jacket design by Carol Devine Carson

Manufactured in the United States of America
First Edition

For Mabon,
and for all the other dogs I have known

# Contents

## Starches: Rice, Grains, Dried Beans, Pasta   100

## Vegetables   133

## Other Voices   147

# Love Me, Feed Me

# Introduction

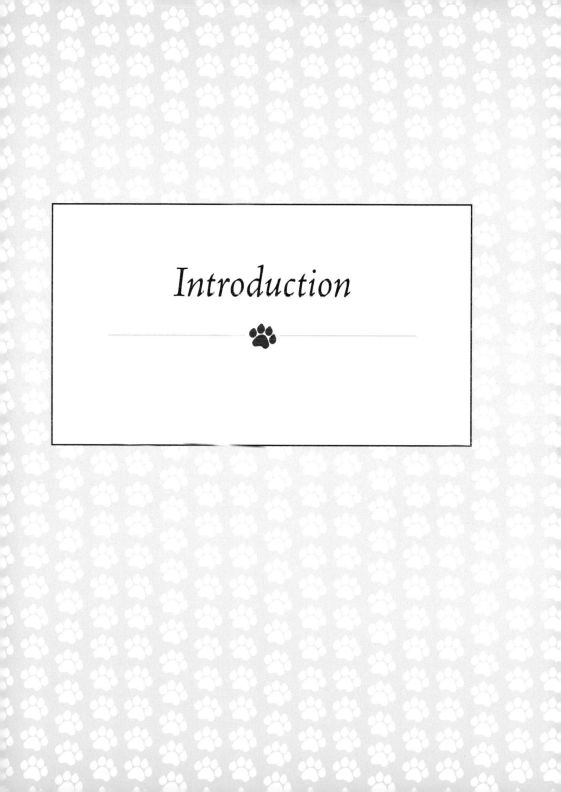

When my Havanese puppy, Mabon, first came to live with me, he was a tiny ball of white fluff, and the ribs enclosing his skinny body were visible. He had only recently been weaned, and his breeders in northern Vermont gave me precise instructions about feeding him half a cup of puppy kibble twice a day. The trouble was that his baby teeth made mere pinpricks on the desiccated pellets, and he would give up trying to chew and swallow them. Clearly he was not getting enough to eat, or perhaps what he was getting wasn't worth his effort.

When we visited the local vet in nearby Danville for final shots, I tentatively asked her what she would think of my cooking for Mabon.* To my delight, she answered that I couldn't do anything better for him, and she gave me a few tips and guidelines. The heart of her message was to trust my instinct and feed him as I would a growing child. So I worked out my own formula: one-third meat, poultry, fish, eggs; one-third fresh vegetables that are good for dogs; one-third starches (rice, pastas, grains, dried beans).

I went home elated. I quickly got out a little frying pan and cooked up some small chunks of the grass-fed beef that my cousin and I are

---

* Incidentally, you'll hear more from this lovely, spirited veterinarian herself on pages 151–152, where, in her own persuasive words, she writes on the benefits of home cooking for your dog.

raising on Stannard Mountain in northern Vermont. I added a couple of lightly cooked young carrots from the garden and some leftover rice I had in the fridge. Watching the way Mabon's nose quivered in anticipation, and how he gobbled up his first good meal, convinced me that this was the way to go, and for more than four years now Mabon has enjoyed a home-cooked supper almost every day.

I think my own love of cooking was born when I was about nine years old and I had my first dog, a Scottie I called Sally MacGregor. I had been longing for a dog, but my parents made me wait until I was old enough to walk her alone on the New York City streets in winter and to feed her. In those days, supermarkets weren't overflowing with canned and dried pet foods, let alone "treats," so feeding an animal meant cooking. But it never seemed like a chore to me. I loved standing at the stove listening to the sizzling sound a few pieces of meat made as I fried them, and enjoying the good smell that rose up from the pan. I liked sharing some of what we were eating with a creature I treasured. It was my way of caring for her.

Now that I am ninety, living alone, I find that part of the fun is in planning a good meal that will please me and that also offers something fresh and nourishing and tasty for Mabon. Just to give an idea of how Mabon and I share our meals, and how I make his food a part of the rhythm of my daily cooking: I might be browsing in the supermarket and come across some ground lamb in a vacuum-sealed package. There is too much meat here for me to consume alone. But I'm tempted—ground lamb is an item not often found in meat counters—so I grab it, sensing that Mabon will like a few lamb burgers as a change from his more usual beef burgers. Also, I have a yen for something with a Middle Eastern flavor, so I will make a few meatballs in a yogurt sauce one night, and maybe a more ambitious dish—a small-sized moussaka that is particularly delicious—another night.

*Good food and treats that his mistress shares with him*

It was experiences like this that led me to keep a log of my cooking for Mabon and me and share the recipes with other pet owners. The more I talked to friends with dogs, the more I sensed that they, too, felt that something was missing in the way they fed their canine friends. But they were apt to be discouraged by their vets, and by what they read in various dog journals about cooking for their pets. Not so Jeffrey Steingarten, who once devoted the monthly feature he writes for *Vogue* magazine to the subject of feeding his newly acquired golden retriever, Sky King. Jeffrey was sizzling up some tasty lamb sausages for himself one night while Sky King looked on hopefully. But all that that poor, hungry dog was given for supper was a bowlful of dry pellets. Finally, he nudged Jeffrey and asked: *Who is the carnivore around here anyway?* From that moment on, Jeffrey cooked for him almost every day. Not just scraps, but beautifully braised short ribs and other carefully prepared delights.

The recipes and suggestions that I have gathered here represent the kinds of dishes that Mabon and I have shared in the years that we have been together. He is clearly a healthy dog with an insatiable appetite. The first thing I ever saw him reject was a piece of overripe banana, which he sniffed at disdainfully and dropped on the floor when I offered it to him. Since then he has joined the ranks of kale haters, and he's not too fond of the broccoli family. The way he eats tells me a lot about his preferences. He always goes for the meat or aromatic fish first, nosing away the veggies and the starch the way a child would.

As to seasoning, I am generally careful, when cooking for the two of us, to hold back on the salt, pepper, and sugar, as well as some items that are considered suspect by dieticians who have made studies of dog nutrition. I'll remove Mabon's portion of dinner when it is ready, and then I'll jazz up mine and finish cooking it. You might well ask whether the flavor of what I am making for myself is compromised. I haven't found it so. Just be careful to taste critically and adjust and taste again, and I'm sure you can satisfy your own palate and at the same time offer your furry friend a purer version that would pass muster with knowledgeable nutritionists.

Clearly I am not an expert. I am guided by common sense and Mabon's responses. I do try to keep up with the latest findings in publications like *The Whole Dog Journal* and *DogWatch*. But I don't want to become obsessive about measuring the nutritional aspect of every bite. I am simply the fond mistress who enjoys cooking for herself and her canine companion, and I hope to persuade you to join the pack. Check with your vet if you have doubts about something you are introducing to your dog's diet and whether a vitamin supplement is recommended.

Aside from the pleasure—and this book is for people who enjoy

cooking—there are several reasons why sharing with your dog makes sense. For one thing, it is in the long run more economical, even though your lucky dog occasionally will be savoring some juicy beef or a rich fillet of salmon or a few nips of ripe, runny cheese. There is no waste, because together you and he will be consuming every last morsel. How frustrating it is in cooking for one when you can't finish up that whole pack of ground turkey before it goes bad.

Some of Mabon's needs have challenged me to be more experimental. I wouldn't ordinarily have bought that pack of rather bland ground turkey. Most grains have proved to be very good for dogs, and I have played with some of the less familiar ones, like farro and quinoa, embellishing them with roast vegetables. There is a whole array of different kinds of rice now on my kitchen shelves, to say nothing of pasta made with flaxseed or buckwheat, instead of the villainous white flour. Mabon is an avid plate-licker, polishing the plates and even some of the pots and pans so clean that I have to remind him, hey, you're only the *pre-wash*.

I also have to think ahead for Mabon, because, once it is suppertime, he is hungry and uses his sharp, insistent bark to get my attention. So I have waiting in the fridge containers of cooked rice, and/or dried beans, polenta, and grits, that I can quickly put to use for the starch component of his dinner.

I can hear the doubters protesting about all the time this must take. But my strategy is to prepare these do-ahead items when I am making them for my own dinner. I will cook a cup or so of rice, eat my relatively modest portion, and store the rest for the week ahead.

Don't let yourself feel guilty if you can't produce that good, well-balanced meal for His or Her Highness every day. You do it for your own pleasure, and there are times when you're running late and

the doggy larder is empty, and you have to fall back on a can or some kibble.

So thank you, Mabon. We are a team. I love having you around when I cook—the way you scratch my leg to remind me it's almost suppertime, then watch my every move in the kitchen, and, when I have your bowl ready, how you dance on your hind legs to reach for it. *At last,* you seem to say, *the best moment of the day!*

# Dogs I Have Known

As a little girl, I was quite afraid of dogs. I remember, when we were staying at my grandmother's house in Montpelier, Vermont, how I would cross the street so I wouldn't have to encounter my aunt's large Irish setter, who only wanted to paw me and lick my face. I knew instinctively, though, that if I really got familiar with a dog, I would no longer be afraid. Finally, my parents were convinced to give it a try, and we acquired six-month-old Sally MacGregor, a cocky little black Scottish terrier who was waiting in a nearby kennel for us to claim her. When we got home, I led her up the stairs in my grandmother's big house; after I shut the door to our room, I found myself enclosed in darkness, as I listened for the sound of a strange creature breathing. After a few whimpers, she fell asleep. But I didn't. Was she all right? When I could hold out no longer, I stumbled out of bed, scooped up MacGregor, and settled her in my bed, where we slept together until morning.

MacGregor quickly became a part of our family. She went everywhere with us, both in Vermont and in Manhattan. So there was no question that she would join us when we decided one Christmas to take the train up to Montpelier to spend the holiday with my grandmother, Nanny.

Nanny had developed a special love for MacGregor. During one of the first years of that little Scottie's life, I had persuaded my parents to let MacGregor and me stay with Nanny through the whole cold winter in Vermont. I promised to work hard at school and get on the honor roll, as my father had always done. Furthermore, I slyly pointed out that they would save a whole year's tuition by sending me to the Montpelier public school. And, most important, MacGregor and I would be good companions for Nanny. (She had a tendency to tipple on the sherry, so they said, when she was alone.) Once again I won them over, and it all worked out as I had hoped. Nanny even bought a big black leather chair, which she placed by the window facing State Street. MacGregor would snuggle there and await my coming the mile and a half home from school, by either foot or bicycle, depending on the weather. The only thing MacGregor didn't share in that winter was the big ice-cream sodas that Nanny and I always had at Jackson's drugstore after we had seen the movie of the week. I always tried to

*The first dog I had when I was a little girl—*
*Sally MacGregor*

make it up to her by cooking something special for her supper when we got home. Nevertheless, she didn't like being separated.

That was what was so particularly painful about what happened on that Christmas visit. When we got to Grand Central Station, we were ushered onto one of the sleeping cars and shown our bunks. But then we were told that our dog *must* travel in the baggage car, and MacGregor was peremptorily pulled away on her leash. I was in tears. But "the law" prevailed, and at that moment the ominous, shrill train whistle blew, and we were off.

When we arrived at Montpelier Junction the next morning, it was still dark, and there was a lot of hustle and bustle all around us as we tried to find the baggage car. Was it up front or in the back? Then, while we were searching, the loud whistle pierced the darkness again, and the train took off, leaving us on the station platform still calling MacGregor. And she was obviously hurtling toward Canada.

I can't recall the details of the next day—only the miraculous moment at the end of the day when the front door downstairs opened and there stood a uniformed man carrying a small, dark, furry bundle. I was at the top of the stairs, and to this day I can still see that little creature with her stubby legs and pointed ears wrestle out of the officer's grasp and climb quickly up the long stairs and into my arms. It was the best Christmas present I ever had.

Alas, we were not so fortunate when, a few years later, our Sally MacGregor was killed by a hit-and-run driver, on the very corner where I used to avoid the Big Dog. I heard her terrifying death cry and knew that she had been hit. There was nothing to do but bring her inside and try to make her comfortable on the warm, familiar kitchen floor. Then, as I stroked her, suddenly she was no longer breathing.

After MacGregor, it was some time before I had another dog, and

*My husband, Evan, and our first dog, Jenny—*
*"her equal would be hard to find"*

my husband, Evan (who was equally endowed with dog-loving genes), always felt there was something missing in our lives. Then, one year, when we had just returned from Europe, Evan and I decided to try spending a winter in New England to see if the country life suited us. Obviously, the experiment would not be complete without a dog. Evan had grown up with a mostly cocker spaniel mutt called Squeers, who loved to lie on the floor with his back legs flattened and splayed out. So we had a soft spot for cocker spaniels and were drawn to a private owner, one of whose dogs had had a litter recently. Happy with our acquisition, we drove the rest of our journey north from New York talking and singing to the golden-haired creature on the seat beside us. I'm sure that's where the name Jenny was born—"Jenny, bright as a penny / Her equal would be hard to find," went the lyrics from a current Broadway hit. But Jenny didn't seem to be respond-

*Evan with his best friend Dilys, our first Welsh terrier*

ing to our high spirits, and we soon realized that she was quite sick and when we gave her her first supper dish, she turned away. So we found a local vet and got some life-saving advice. "Tempt her with something so strong-tasting and oily and smelly that she can't resist eating it, such as sardines. Then give her a little more—and more." Sure enough, the sardines did the trick, and she lived a good life thereafter.

After Jenny came our first Welsh terrier, whom we named Dilys in honor of Evan's Welsh roots. Her only flaw was that she would go berserk when enclosed in moving spaces such as an elevator or an automobile. Finally, in desperation, when the elevator man in our apartment building in New York refused to ride with Dilys, we called in a dog behaviorist. After offering a few theories about why Dilys might be so crazed—one of them being that she was the only female in a litter of six

*Dilys*

and the last to be born—our expert behaviorist suggested that we all get in a taxi together so that he could observe Dilys's behavior. Dilys performed as expected, flinging herself against the divide that protected the driver, and growling fiercely if we tried to touch her. The poor doc was terrified and pleaded to have the driver pull over and let him out.

Probably all Dilys really needed was some good home-cooked food, but I was still enslaved to the dog-food industry then. And she did calm down as she aged.

After our first experience with a Welshie, we were determined to try again. We had found a highly recommended breeder who seemed very proud of the puppy she had selected for us (the pup had just won a blue ribbon in the local dog show). The little dog settled into our car comfortably, bonding with her new masters, as we made the long drive to northern Vermont. Evan had brought along a list he made of possible names for her, but it wasn't until we drove up the steep hill to the house we were renting, sight unseen, for the summer that we settled on Teg. The word *teg,* which means "beautiful" in Welsh, was not only fitting but seemed to have some powerful connection to this perfect little creature sitting beside us. It was also short and easy for us to pronounce (not typical of Welsh words). And then we fell in love with the house perched on a steep hill with a 180-degree view of the Green Mountains. We immediately started calling the place "Bryn Teg," which means "Beautiful Hill."

A couple of years later, Evan had an assignment to do a story on

Wales, so we worked out an itinerary that would include stopping at the village where his grandparents had lived, which we had never seen. As we were walking around, a man came out of one of the small stone houses, still chewing the cabbage he'd had for lunch, and asked if he could be of help. When Evan explained that he was looking for his grandparents' home, the man told him that their farm was a mile up the hill, and all that was left was the foundation. "But you can find them in the cemetery," he added. And he pointed us there, describing how Evan's grandmother used to walk the long mile down the hill to attend chapel, carrying a little dog under her arm. Then, suddenly, I saw Evan stop in front of one of the gravestones and peer at it to read the inscription; from the expression on his face, I thought he had seen a ghost. The gravestone read:

WILLIAM AND MARY JONES

BRYN TEG

Later on I tell the story of Teg's final days and how Madoc, who preceded Mabon, took care of her. I am ashamed to admit that Madoc's more notable claim to fame is that he had the audacity to nip Jane Goodall, who had come to see me to discuss a book project. Despite my warning, she stroked him on the vulnerable spot behind his ears, and he didn't like it.

My stories of dogs that we have cherished would not be complete without the sad tales of Briar and Precious.

After our first experience with a Welsh terrier, Evan became interested in border terriers, who look much like the Welshie but are a little smaller and tougher, as you can see from the photograph on page 24. The only trouble was that, once we acquired Briar and brought her to the city, the only place she would pee was on Park Avenue. She preferred the greensward in the middle of the avenue with its grass and soft earth. Many were the nights when Evan or I would climb with her over the iron fence that led there and then wait—often to no avail. Sadly, she did not have enough time to outgrow this misdemeanor, because she was stricken with the deadly parvovirus and did not survive.

Precious was another story. He was a little mutt I got from a Long Island shelter, and I never should have brought him home. But my apartment seemed so empty after Evan died and then Madoc's time was up; I persuaded myself that I could rescue this miserable creature, who was being displayed in a trailer filled with kennels outside FAO Schwarz. The trouble was that the little dog I dragged home was terrified of the city and flung herself on the sidewalk trembling as trucks roared by and sirens screamed. And it did not get any better when I got her home and named her Precious. She would huddle under the bed, and I had to drag her out, and all the tender, loving care I had hoped to give her was in vain. I didn't give up for a month, and when I finally had to return her to the shelter, I begged them to find her a home that was on a quiet street with green grass around, far from the roar of the city. I think of you often, Precious, and hope you found someone to love you and feed you well.

Another dog I'll never forget is Nikki, a caramel-colored, medium-sized poodle who was a visitor in the apartment in Paris where I was staying in the late 1940s. When a few of us decided we wanted to drive to Provence, we took Nikki along (in France dogs could go anywhere).

As we drove south, we saw, near Vienne, a billboard promoting din-

*Our border terrier Briar*

ing at La Pyramide. Why not try it? We were famished, and it was getting late. The gateway and garden leading to the restaurant looked very elegant, and we were mortified when a huge man in chef's garb appeared just as Nikki was relieving herself. But to our surprise, the chef threw open his arms and welcomed us, bestowing a special kiss on Nikki's brow. Once he had seated us inside and assured us that we were his guests, out came one delicious course after another, with Nikki always getting her fair share. We later learned that this large and generous man was Fernand Point, one of the most famous chefs in France at the time. So thank you, Nikki, for an experience that, I think, changed my life.

## Do's and Don'ts for Little Dogs

When I brought Mabon down from Vermont to his winter home in New York City, he was devastated that he couldn't run free. Then I learned that before 9:00 a.m. Central Park welcomed unleashed dogs, so I thought all would be well. Mabon was so ecstatic to be on the grass again, and he quivered with excitement as the unleashed dogs raced by. However, though he looked at me with imploring eyes, I knew that I should not unleash him because he would not come when I called. I held out. That is, until an important-looking guy—I think he was a trainer—turned to me and asked why I didn't let my little dog off the leash. "He'll run with the

*"Socializing" in Central Park*

pack," he said confidently. "And if he doesn't, I'll go after him." So I trusted him and snapped off the leash. Mabon took off like a thunderbolt, outrunning the big Labs and the swift borzois, and soon he was out of sight, heading toward the parkway, where the cars zipped by at a dangerous speed. I kept calling—to no avail. And where was the friendly trainer when I needed him? He was in sight, but he wasn't budging. Finally, I sat down on a rock and cried. Then who should appear but a happy, exhausted little white dog, looking very pleased with himself.

- Don't be tempted to feed your dog from the table where you eat. You are simply inviting him to be a nuisance. I'm all for his help in licking the plates after a meal, but put them discreetly on the floor, away from your dining area.

- Do try to have separate dinner hours. Mabon has his supper around four, following our afternoon walk. He has had only a small handful of kibble or a few puppy biscuits for breakfast, usually after a romp in the park, so he is hungry.

- Do be sure to warm up your dog's supper if you are feeding him something ice-cold from the fridge. I often warm things in the microwave, and I am convinced that Mabon thinks there is a cook inside of this strange humming machine, tending to his dinner. He will sit in front of it, barking impatiently and batting the window with his paw, until the bell goes off. The same thing happens if I slip a bowlful of something too hot into the freezer to chill. Now, how did that chef get into the freezer?

- Watch out for antifreeze. Only a lick or two of it, which someone carelessly splashed on the ground, can be dangerous, so call your veterinarian immediately if your dog has lapped any of it up.

- In big cities, if the little door at the base of the tall lamps that line the streets has been carelessly left open, your male dog is tempted to lift his leg and leave his mark. If his aim is good, he, alas, could be electrocuted.

- Button batteries, if swallowed, are particularly toxic and should be disposed of carefully. That is best done by returning the used batteries to the place where you bought them.

# The Recipes

Here are some recipes for dishes that I have shared with Mabon. I am starting with meats, poultry, fish, and eggs not only because they furnish essential proteins in his diet, but also because they are the foods he seems to love best.

The next section draws on the wide world of starch accompaniments: rice, pasta, dried beans (known as pulses), and healthy grains.

My discussion of vegetables consists mostly of guidance in the preparation and cooking of vegetables that are good (or not so good) for dogs, based mostly on my own experiences plus a little help from nutritionists.

*Bon appétit, mes petits chiens.*

# Meats, Poultry, Eggs, and Fish

## A Word About Portion Size

These recipes are designed to serve one person of modest appetite plus a small dog. Mabon is a Havanese, which is considered a small breed, and he is allotted only one brimming cup of food a day plus a little kibble or treat to get going in the morning.

If you have a larger dog, or several, in your household, you can use these recipes—just multiply the amounts. Recipes are only guidelines anyway. And dogs have different metabolisms. Anyone who has seen Mabon streak across the meadow or run from one end of the apartment to the other tossing pillows in the air nonstop would know that this pup had a terrific appetite. You can also find some useful tips in the stories that some of my friends have contributed at the back of this book.

*This photograph gives an idea of the relative size of
Mabon's portion and my portion.*

# Roast Beef Shoulder with Broccoli Rabe

The grass-fed beef that we are raising in northern Vermont will yield a shoulder that can serve Mabon and me for a couple of meals. By roasting the potatoes and vegetables alongside, you will make a delicious meal with the right proportion of meat, starch, and vegetable. I have chosen to use broccoli rabe rather than broccoli here because it comes in a more modest size, so we are not forced to eat broccoli all week. Roasting gives the more delicate plant a lovely flavor and texture, and Mabon will usually eat it.

THE RUB

1 fat garlic clove, smashed, peeled, then minced with a little salt

A few turns of the pepper mill
1 teaspoon grated fresh ginger

1 small shoulder of beef, about 1¼ pounds
3 or 4 new potatoes, each

peeled and sliced into 3 or 4 lengthwise pieces
1 bunch broccoli rabe

Mix the rub ingredients together, and then spread them over both sides of
the beef. Put the meat in a roasting pan, and strew the potatoes and broccoli rabe all around. Roast in a preheated 350-degree oven for 30 minutes,
turning the meat and the vegetables over once. Let rest 5 minutes before
slicing.

You won't use all the broccoli rabe, but cook it
anyway. It's good in a salad, in an omelet, or in a
soup. Any leftover meat is delicious cold.

# Braised Beef Shanks

Our share of the grass-fed beef shanks from the cows we are raising in northern Vermont comes to us frozen and wrapped four to a package—a hefty amount for just me and a twelve-pound-plus Havanese pup. But you need good-sized shanks to get a fair share of that delicious treasure—the marrow embedded in the bone. I use a small grapefruit spoon to get at that unctuous treat, and Mabon uses his tongue, and it's hard to tell who does the most efficient job. I warn you, though: line your kitchen floor with newspapers for your dog to work on his shank bone, unless, of course, you are in the country. I've been known to take the bone for Mabon to Central Park, where he can lie on the grass and gnaw on it until it is licked clean. Watch your dog as he gnaws on a bone, and if he is doing it too vigorously, take the bone away. Mabon usually puts the bone away when he's had enough.

4 hefty beef shanks, preferably from grass-fed beef, about 3 inches thick
Salt and freshly ground pepper
1 tablespoon light olive oil or vegetable oil
1 large onion, peeled and sliced
Beef broth, as needed
1 fat garlic clove, smashed and peeled
A handful of fresh Italian parsley
1 bay leaf
2 large carrots, peeled and cut into chunks
Gremolata (optional—see box)

Remove excess fat from the shanks, and rub salt and pepper over all sides of them. Heat the oil in a heavy pot just large enough to accommodate the four shanks lying flat. Brown them on all sides. Remove them to a plate while you cook the onion until limp and lightly browned. Return the shanks to the pot. Add the beef broth. Scatter in the garlic, parsley, bay leaf, and carrots, and cook over low heat for about 1½ hours.

Test now by piercing the meat with a fork. If it is meltingly tender, it is done. Serve yourself a generous portion of the beef shanks, and sprinkle some gremolata on top. The raw garlic and seasoning might be too much for your dog, but you can serve him the beef shank plain. You'll have more than enough beef for yourself and your hungry companion, so give it another round during the week ahead, using it perhaps as a sauce for pasta for one evening.

## Gremolata

I find this gremolata very useful to have around, particularly when I have cut down on the amount of garlic I have used in cooking the dish. The verdict is not yet in on whether garlic is harmful to dogs, but if you want to play it safe, you'll withhold the garlic from your dog and treat yourself to a sprinkling of this gremolata to spice up your serving.

Peel of ¼ lemon, finely chopped
1 fat garlic clove, smashed, peeled, and chopped very fine with a little salt mashed in

A small handful of fresh Italian parsley leaves, chopped

Toss the ingredients together, and sprinkle on the meat.

Good news. The latest findings tell us that garlic is good for dogs and should be made a part of their diet. After all, humans and animals have been consuming it in various forms for four thousand years, and recent research studies find that garlic helps fight cancer and rebuild the immune system. And it is not just internal consumption that is recommended but the dried varieties of garlic (one is known as Bug Off Garlic) that are highly effective at repelling ticks and fleas and deerflies. For more information, check the Internet.

# Beef Sirloin Flap

The sirloin flap is a thin piece of meat that I like to sear quickly and then let rest while I toss a few scallions into the pan and sizzle them in a little butter and beef broth to pour over my portion of steak. Mabon and I usually take a walk about mid-afternoon when we are in Vermont, and it is fun to be on the lookout for wild things that can add to our dinners, such as colorful chive flowers, which I can sprinkle over my steak.

A small splash of light olive oil
1 beef sirloin flap or hanger steak, preferably grass-fed, about 8–10 ounces
Salt and freshly ground pepper
2 teaspoons unsalted butter
2 or 3 scallions, including tender green parts, roughly chopped

2 or 3 tablespoons beef broth, plus a splash of red wine, if wanted
A sprinkling of chopped fresh chives or chive flowers or, if not easily available, fresh parsley

You'll probably have to cut the long flap into three pieces to make it fit in a medium-sized skillet. Rub the pan lightly with olive oil, and heat it up. Meanwhile, cut the long flap steak into three pieces, and rub them lightly with salt and pepper. When the pan is sizzling hot (but not smoking), lay in the steaks and sear them on both sides. If you are using grass-fed beef, the flap is apt to be very thin, and the searing should take less than a minute.

Remove the meat from the pan to a warm plate, and melt the butter in the hot pan. When it is sizzling, toss in the scallions along with the splash of broth and/or wine. Pour the garnish of chives on top of the people portion. Mabon gets his unadorned.

# Scrap Soup

One day when Julia Child and Jacques Pépin were doing their last television series together in Julia's kitchen, I could tell Jacques was upset about something, and I asked him what was the matter. In a typical French gesture, he shook his fingers as though to dismiss something unpleasant, and admitted that he hated to see such waste—all those good things going into the garbage. In his kitchen, he said, he would fill up big, empty milk cartons with all the scraps; nothing went unused. When he had a couple of well-stuffed frozen cartons, he would empty the contents into a pot of water and let it all simmer away until he had a rich, delicious (and mysterious) broth.

I have recently learned that vegetable essence is particularly good for home-fed dogs. So I started to emulate Jacques. Now I always have a stash of frozen scraps hidden away in my freezer, and I cook up a new batch of soup whenever the supply is running low. Not only is it a good way to give Mabon those essential vitamins, but a little of the warm concentrated soup heats up the ice-cold leftovers that are part of his supper. And, of course, I get to share some of Mabon's potage, spicing it up with salt and pepper, some grated cheese, and yesterday's bread. (Incidentally, the rind of a hunk of tired Parmigiano, which you were about to get rid of, is delicious in scrap soup.)

# Lamb or Beef Meatballs with Yogurt Sauce

This is the dish I secretly longed for, as I mentioned in the introduction; when I saw the package of ground lamb in the supermarket, I knew I had to make it for Mabon and me.

2 tablespoons fresh breadcrumbs
About ½ pound ground lamb or beef
1 teaspoon beaten egg (see page 79)
Pinch of cinnamon
Pinch of allspice
1 tablespoon chopped fresh parsley
1 fat garlic clove, peeled and finely chopped
Salt and freshly ground pepper to taste
½ teaspoon light olive oil or vegetable oil
½ cup plain yogurt, at room temperature

Pour a little water over the breadcrumbs, and let them soak until the water is absorbed. Squeeze the breadcrumbs and discard the water. Mix the crumbs with the meat, egg, cinnamon, allspice, parsley, garlic, and salt and pepper to taste. Squish everything together to mix well, then form into six meatballs about the size of golf balls. Heat the oil in a medium frying pan, and slip the meatballs in. Fry slowly, turning to brown lightly on all sides, and cover for the last half of cooking time (about 15 minutes for lamb, or 10 minutes for beef). Pour the yogurt over the meatballs. Cook just enough to warm the sauce, and serve with rice.

# Grass-Fed Beef Tongue

Among my allotment of Bryn Teg grass-fed beef this year was the tongue, which I always love. And I knew Mabon would help me eat it. Actually, it was not very big—about 1¼ pounds—so I figured it wouldn't take as long to cook as the usual beef tongue.

FOR THE PARBOILING

1 grass-fed beef tongue
1 onion, quartered

2 or 3 garlic cloves, peeled and
  sliced
2 celery stalks

FOR THE BRAISING

1 tablespoon vegetable oil
¼ cup Madeira

Salt and freshly ground pepper
1½ cups beef broth

FOR THE VEGETABLE GARNISH

1 parsnip, peeled and cut into
  2-inch chunks
2 white turnips, peeled and cut
  into half-moon slices about
  ½ inch thick

2 medium-sized carrots, peeled
  and cut into 2-inch chunks
3 or 4 new potatoes, partially
  peeled

Parboil the tongue with the parboiling vegetables for 1 hour. Remove the tongue and aromatic vegetables from the cooking water. When the tongue is cool enough to handle, using a sharp knife, scrape and peel away the tough skin.

Heat the oil in a heavy pot big enough to accommodate the trimmed tongue. Add the aromatic vegetables, and sauté them for a few minutes. Place the tongue on top of the vegetables, splash in the Madeira, and cook down a little. Salt and pepper lightly. Add the beef broth, bring to a boil, then cover with foil and a tight-fitting lid. Braise in a preheated 325-degree

oven for about 50 minutes. Now add the vegetable garnishes, and braise in the oven for 30 more minutes. Correct the seasoning of your portion. You and your pup will get more than one supper each out of this. Tongue is delicious cold in a salad, and it makes a great sandwich.

# Cream Sauce or Béchamel

It's always good to have a little cream sauce tucked away in the freezer. It is used so often in American home cooking, but we frequently skip over a recipe that calls for it, particularly if we're cooking for just one person and a dog. The solution is simple. When you are making the batch that is called for in a recipe, just make double, triple, or even quadruple the amount, and then freeze what you don't use immediately in 1-cup or even smaller containers, carefully marked. So here's my formula, which yields almost 4 cups.

| | |
|---|---|
| 6 tablespoons butter | ½ teaspoon salt, or more to |
| 6 tablespoons all-purpose | taste |
| flour | Freshly ground pepper |
| 3 cups milk, or more as | Several gratings of nutmeg |
| needed | |

Heat the butter in a heavy saucepan. When the butter is melted, stir in the flour and cook over low heat for 3 minutes, stirring. Remove from the heat, and when the bubbles have died out, pour in all of the milk and whisk thoroughly. Return the saucepan to medium heat, and keep whisking, carefully scraping up the thickening sauce from the bottom of the pan. Add the salt and pepper and a couple of gratings of nutmeg. Let the sauce continue to cook over very gentle heat, stirring now and then, until it is the thickness you wish.

Voilà, it is done. Incidentally, I often speak French to Mabon when I cook. He likes the lilting sound of it and doesn't try to correct my accent.

# Shepherd's Beef or Lamb Pie

This is one of those old, homey dishes designed to give leftovers a new life. It's usually made with yesterday's lamb roast and can be rather plain and dry. But if you use a braised meat, you will have its delicious sauce to keep the ingredients moist and flavorful. I also like to insert one or two fresh ingredients to liven up the dish—hence the leek and a few mushrooms.

1 large russet baking potato
2 tablespoons milk or cream
1 teaspoon butter
3 or 4 medium-sized mushrooms, quartered
A few 1-inch slices of leek, thoroughly washed
About 1¾–2 cups small pieces of braised beef or other cooked meat

About 2 tablespoons braising juice, along with whatever aromatic braising vegetables might be left over
Salt and freshly ground pepper to taste
A sprinkling of grated cheese

Peel the potato and cut into large chunks. Boil the potato in water to cover until tender when pierced with a fork. Drain and peel while still warm, and mash with the milk or cream. If it is a really large potato, you'll need only about three-quarters of it (put the rest away for another use). Melt the butter in a small frying pan, scatter in the mushrooms and leek, and cook 3 or 4 minutes. I remove about ⅓ cup of the braised meat to a smaller bowl for Mabon. Put the rest, and the braising liquid and vegetables, into a baking dish, season with salt and pepper to taste, and top with the mashed potato. Bake in a preheated 350-degree oven for 20 minutes. Now sprinkle on the cheese and return the dish to the oven, turning up the heat to brown the top a little, or slip the dish under the broiler.

I usually give Mabon's share a sweet potato topping rather than mashed white potato, because it's better for him—and he loves the sweetness. I try to roast a couple of good-sized sweet potatoes when I'm roasting something else, so I have them ready at hand. Then, when I'm about to make his shepherd's pie, I warm his potato portion and mash it with a little butter. I spread this topping over the braised meat. This also makes a wonderful baked dish for human consumption.

*A standoff:*
*Mabon encountering one of our Angus bulls*

# Calves' Liver and Bacon

Mabon has never turned up his nose at innards. Like me, he seems to love the strong, earthy flavor of liver, and bacon is always an extra treat.

2 strips bacon
2 teaspoons butter
2 slices of liver, preferably calves' liver

Flour for dredging
Salt and freshly ground pepper
1 shallot, peeled and sliced thin
A good splash of red wine

Cook the bacon slowly in a skillet just big enough to accommodate the liver slices. When the bacon pieces are done, press out excess fat with a spatula and put the slices on a paper towel to drain. Pour off the bacon fat, and add the butter to the skillet. While the butter is heating, dredge the liver in flour, and salt and pepper lightly. Slip the liver into the pan. Cook about 1½–2 minutes on each side, depending on how thick the slices are (you want the interior rosy). Add the shallot, splash the wine into the pan, and cook down until syrupy. (Eliminate this last step for your dog.) Now pour the sauce over the liver, and enjoy with crisp bacon.

# Stir-Fry of Pork, Seasonal Vegetables, and Almonds

The secret to a good stir-fry is to have all the ingredients ready and lined up in order of use before you start cooking.

**THE MARINADE**

2 teaspoons soy sauce
2 teaspoons dry sherry
Pinch of sugar

2 teaspoons cornstarch
dissolved in 2 tablespoons
water

**THE SAUCE**

2 teaspoons oyster sauce
1 teaspoon soy sauce
2 teaspoons dry sherry

Pinch of sugar
1 teaspoon toasted
sesame oil

1 cup narrow 2-inch-long logs of
pork, preferably from the loin
or tenderloin

2 teaspoons vegetable oil
1 large garlic clove, smashed and
peeled
2 quarter-sized slices of fresh
ginger, peeled
¼ green or red bell pepper,
cut into logs like the
pork
2 slices turnip, peeled and cut
into logs

½ small zucchini, quartered
lengthwise and cut into logs
1 medium-sized carrot, peeled
and cut into thin sticks
3 scallions, including tender
green parts, trimmed of tough
outer leaves and cut into
2-inch logs
¼ cup chicken broth
¼ cup sliced almonds (optional)

Mix the marinade ingredients together in a small bowl. Do the same with the sauce ingredients, and set aside. Toss the pork in the marinade, coating well, then let marinate, refrigerated, for 30 minutes. Heat 1 teaspoon of the oil in a wok, if you have one, or a medium-sized heavy pan. When the oil is almost smoking, toss in the garlic and ginger, then the pork, and sear quickly over high heat. Remove the contents to a plate, and keep warm. Pour the remaining oil into the wok, and when hot, toss in the bell pepper, turnip, zucchini, and carrot. Stir-fry for about 30 seconds. Now add the scallions and broth, cover, and let steam until the vegetables are just tender; they should still have some crunch. Pour in the sauce, and stir-fry quickly to heat through. Scatter the almonds, if using, on top.

## Too Spicy for Your Dog?

If your dog has a tender tummy, skip the garlic and the ginger and just extract about a quarter of the meat and vegetables, then stir-fry them in a little oil until they are cooked through. Play with new flavors until they seem right for your dog. He'll tell you. I have also learned that almonds are not good for dogs, so just leave them out and try a few pine nuts instead. And spinach has recently been demoted! But that doesn't mean that all dogs are allergic. Test a new ingredient, offering just a small taste the first few times.

# Pork and Leek au Gratin

This delectable dish of a few thick slices of leftover pork (tenderloin is best) over a bed of leeks perfectly fits our formula of meat protein, a small portion of starch (the new potatoes), and an abundance of leeks for the vegetable, with a topping of crumbs and a little cheese. My recipe, as I said earlier, is for one person of modest appetite, but if you want to have some for your ever-eager and hungry friend, just add another one-quarter the amount to all the ingredients.

2 or 3 leeks, white part only, cut into ½-inch pieces and rinsed
1 tablespoon butter
2 or 3 small new potatoes, cut into ½-inch slices
⅓ cup water

Salt and freshly ground pepper
2 tablespoons heavy cream
4 slices cooked pork tenderloin
2 tablespoons fresh breadcrumbs
2 tablespoons grated Parmesan cheese

Sauté the leeks in butter a minute or so, then add the potato slices and water. Salt and pepper lightly, and sauté gently, about 10 minutes, covered, checking to see that the water hasn't boiled away. When the vegetables are tender, add the cream. Transfer half the mixture to a gratin dish, lay the pork slices on top, and salt and pepper again. Top with the remaining leeks and potatoes, cover loosely with foil, and bake in a preheated 350 degree oven for 20 minutes. Remove the foil, and sprinkle the breadcrumbs and cheese on top. Return the dish to the oven, and bake 5–10 minutes, until lightly browned on top.

Save the leek greens for scrap soup
(see page 37).

# Pork and Ham Croquettes

Every so often, I get a nostalgic pang for some particular food from my childhood. It's probably a taste or a smell that brought on the memory, but the urge to recapture it is so compelling that I have to get to the kitchen and, guided by memory only, try to re-create that dish. I always like introducing Mabon to new food experiences, even if they won't linger with him in quite the same way. Or will they?

½ cup ground ham
½ cup ground cooked pork
¾ cup cream sauce or béchamel (see page 43)
1 teaspoon Dijon mustard
1 tablespoon chopped mixed fresh herbs, such as tarragon or sage along with parsley and chives, or about ½ teaspoon dried herbs

2 scallions, including tender green parts, trimmed and chopped
Salt and freshly ground pepper to taste
¾ cup fresh breadcrumbs
1 egg, beaten
Vegetable oil, for frying

Mix together the ground ham and pork, the cream sauce, mustard, herbs, and scallions and season to taste with a little salt and pepper, squishing them with your fingers until they are well blended. Or you can whirl everything together in a food processor—pulsing, so that the mixture doesn't become mush. Chill in the refrigerator for at least 30 minutes. Meanwhile, line up the breadcrumbs and egg to make the crust. Remove the croquette mixture from the fridge, and form into three cylinder shapes approximately 2½ inches long. Chill them again for 20 minutes or longer, until firm enough to handle. Roll them first in the breadcrumbs, then the egg, and finally in the crumbs again. Have a small skillet heating with enough oil in it to come halfway up the sides of the croquets. When the oil is hot but not smoking, lower two or three croquettes carefully into the sizzling oil. After browning on both sides, turn the heat down and continue cooking for about 2 minutes, turning often. No embellishment is needed, but Mabon would get a leafy green vegetable and/or some peas or lima beans. And, oh, that first bite—the crunchy hot crumbs, and the burst of flavor as the warm, spicy ham/pork mince oozes over the crust.

Any leftover egg can just be stirred into whatever cooked dish Mabon may be having.

"Guests are coming, and I'm not going to beg for food!"

# Braised Lamb Shoulder Chops

If the chops come shrink-wrapped, two to a package, that's too much for me, so Mabon gets most of the second braised chop. And there is still a little left over.

1 tablespoon light olive oil or vegetable oil
2 lamb shoulder chops
Salt and freshly ground pepper to taste
Pinch of dried rosemary
1 medium-sized onion, peeled and cut into generous slices
1 garlic clove, peeled and sliced thin
Splash of red wine
About ¼ cup beef broth
Fresh parsley sprigs

Heat the olive oil in a medium-sized ovenproof dish, and brown the chops on both sides. Season with a little salt, pepper, and rosemary, and toss in the onion slices and garlic. Add a splash of red wine and the beef broth, and strew the parsley sprigs on top. Lay a sheet of parchment over the contents of the pan, then cover with foil, and finally set the tight fitting lid on top. Then braise in a preheated 325-degree oven for 45 minutes. Discard the parsley sprigs.

The leftover lamb may go into a casserole (see lamb with dried beans, page 123) or a pasta.

I learned the trick of covering the pan this way from Scott Peacock and Edna Lewis, and it is effective at keeping the juices intact and intensifying the flavor of the meat.

# Lamb and Sweet Potato Hash

Here is an example of borrowing from Mabon's hoard of sweet potatoes to create a wonderful hash. I got the idea of combining white and sweet potatoes from David Nussbaum, a food writer and editor from Massachusetts. When a reporter once asked him what his favorite food was, David answered without hesitation: potatoes. He also has a way with dogs. My dogs have always gone crazy when they recognized his footsteps a full city block away. See page 159 for David's take on treats.

¼ red or yellow bell pepper
1 slice of a fennel bulb, or 1 rib of celery
2 scallions, including the fresh green part, or ¼ small onion
1 tablespoon butter
1 medium-sized new potato, boiled or roasted until tender

2–3-inch hunk of roasted sweet potato
Leftover lamb shoulder, enough to make 1 cup chopped, including any pan juice
Salt and freshly ground pepper to taste
A sprinkling of chopped fresh Italian parsley

Cut the bell pepper, fennel or celery, and scallions or onion into small dice. Melt the butter in a small frying pan, and toss in the vegetables. Cook slowly for about 5 minutes. Meanwhile, peel and cut up the potatoes, and add them to the other vegetables along with the chopped meat and its juice. Let cook slowly, semi-covered, shaking the pan, until the vegetables begin to brown. Now pour in the liquid (see opposite). Turn the hash over, scraping up any browned bits, and cook until the liquid is absorbed. Brown the other side. I put about a third of the hash into Mabon's bowl, then I salt and pepper my own portion and crown it with chopped parsley.

"There's nothing like a snooze after a good meal."

You should include at least ¼ cup of flavorful
braising sauce. If you have none, use beef broth.
It helps to bring a glaze to your hash.

# Moussaka

The idea of my making my version of this classic Greek dish just to feed me and my dog may seem a bit much. But I find cooking deeply satisfying. Not only is it a challenge to get it right, but it is relaxing to chop and stir and taste and adjust. So often the smell of the cooking will evoke a memory, such as how my mother would try to persuade us that eggplant was not really a vegetable but, breaded and fried British style, it could almost be the meat course on our meatless-dinner night. It took biting into my first moussaka and tasting the lovely marriage of lamb and olive-oil-coated slices of grilled eggplant to know the truth.

2 teaspoons light olive oil or
   vegetable oil
1 small onion or 1 medium-sized
   shallot, finely chopped
1 cup shredded leftover braised
   lamb (see page 55)
½ teaspoon cinnamon
½ teaspoon sugar
Pinch of chili powder
Sprinkle of chopped fresh parsley

Salt and freshly ground pepper
   to taste
1 large tomato, chopped, or
   ½ cup tomato sauce
1 small or ½ medium-sized
   eggplant
Olive oil, for brushing
½ cup cream sauce or béchamel
   (see page 43)

Heat the light olive oil, and in a small pan sauté the chopped onion or shallot until translucent. Meanwhile, put the shredded lamb in a mixing bowl, and squish it with your fingers. Sprinkle in the cinnamon, sugar, chili powder, parsley, and a little salt and pepper. Continue to mix with your hands, breaking up the meat, then dump the contents of the bowl into the pan with the golden onion. Add the tomato or sauce, and let simmer 5 minutes very gently. Set aside.

Cut the eggplant into ⅓-inch slices. Brush generously with olive oil, and sprinkle lightly with salt. Broil about 8 inches from the heat until golden and speckled, then turn the slices over and broil the other side.

Now the assembly: Take half the slices of grilled eggplant and line the bottom of a single-portion baking dish with them. Distribute the meat mixture on top, then make a final layer of the remaining eggplant; pour the cream sauce over all, distributing it evenly. Bake in a preheated 375-degree oven for 30 minutes.

Most of this will go to me, but Mabon has gotten a few licks and seems to like it.

## Eggplant: An Acquired Taste?

I think the taste for eggplant grew on Mabon, which shows that a dog's appreciation for unfamiliar foods can be encouraged. I have found that if I give him the flesh of the rounder stem end of the eggplant, he appreciates it more, and that's because it is relatively seedless. We are advised to scrape the seeds out of tomatoes and other fruit if we are feeding them to our dogs. Also, eggplant can be bitter, and sprinkling slices with salt and then, after 30 minutes or so, patting the pieces dry can make a difference.

# A Whole Chicken

Why not get a whole chicken for the week ahead? It's more economical to cook this way, and the chicken is fresher tasting. It also offers you a challenge to be creative and come up with some tasty chicken dishes to share with your canine companion.

Try to get a smallish, decently raised roasting chicken—about 3–3¼ pounds—and check to see if it comes with a packet of giblets (if not, complain and try to find one that does). It should contain the liver, heart, gizzard, and neck. The liver, which I consider the cook's treat, is too small to be shared with Mabon, alas, but just the right size for me to tuck into my shirred-egg dish for a very special Sunday breakfast (see page 80). In compensation, Mabon gets in his supper bowl the heart and gizzard, just cooked through. If your dog is persnickety, don't waste these treasures on him; toss them, along with the neck, into the chicken stock you'll be making; they add a depth of flavor.

Now cut the whole carcass up. Detailed instructions, along with illustra-

tions, appear in any number of cookbooks you probably have, so I'll skip the details here. Anyway, it's fun to work out your own method. I find that boning shears are very helpful in cutting out the backbone, rather than whacking it with a cleaver. What you want are eight pieces (a breast piece from either side, two drumsticks, two thighs, and two wings) for yourself and your little friend, who will be watching this whole procedure carefully, hoping that you will drop a wing on the floor for him. So be careful not to (small, splintery bones can be killers). I like to cook the dark meat, lightly painted with a marinade and brushed with a secret ingredient (a touch of dark Vermont maple syrup), on the grill or under the broiler. Then, for another meal, I'll sauté the breast gently in butter and finish with a delicate sauce. Or, if I have a trayful of roasted vegetables, I'll bake the chicken with the fresh roasted vegetables nestled in among them. So here are several recipes for you to play with and share with your grateful dog.

# Grilled or Broiled
# Chicken Legs and Thighs

I prefer the dark meat of the chicken for both broiling and grilling. I leave the skin on and brush it with a little maple syrup, which makes it nice and crisp with an elusive flavor. Also, when I'm eating, I like picking up the drumstick with my fingers if I can stand Mabon's longing look as I gnaw on the bones. He gets his share with his supper, but, alas, boneless.

2 teaspoons white wine vinegar
1 tablespoon light olive oil or
    vegetable oil
Salt to taste

4 pieces dark meat chicken
    (2 thighs, 2 drumsticks)
1 tablespoon maple syrup,
    preferably dark

Mix together in a bowl the vinegar, oil, and a pinch of salt. Drop in the four chicken pieces, and toss them by hand in the bowl until they are just lightly coated. Refrigerate for ½ hour or longer (even overnight). When ready to cook, preheat your grill or broiler. Paint the surface of the chicken with a light coating of maple syrup, and grill or broil for 12 to 15 minutes; if you're using the broiler, the chicken pieces should be about 5 or 6 inches from the heat. Turn once or twice (and don't let you-know-who snatch a piece from the rack). Test for doneness by pricking deeply into the flesh; the juices should run clear.

# Chicken Pieces with Seasonal Vegetables

If you are feeding a very hungry dog, include some of the breast meat in this sauté. I love the skin and try to keep it crispy by pan-sautéing the vegetables separately and then combining the two, rather than drowning the browned chicken pieces in the moist veggies.

3 teaspoons light olive oil or
    vegetable oil
1 chicken drumstick and thigh
    and half the breast
1 shallot, peeled and thinly sliced
A splash of white wine or dry
    vermouth or chicken broth
¼ large red bell pepper, seeds
    removed, sliced into long, thin
    pieces

3 medium-sized mushrooms,
    each cut into 4 or 5 slices
1 cup small pieces of broccoli
    florets separated into small
    pieces, and stems peeled and
    julienned
Salt and freshly ground pepper
    to taste
A sprinkling of fresh chopped
    herbs, such as Italian parsley,
    tarragon, and basil

Heat 1 teaspoon of the oil in a medium frying pan, and when it's sizzling, drop in the chicken pieces. Lower the heat a little, and brown the chicken pieces well, turning them several times. After cooking about 5 minutes on each side, scatter the shallot into the pan and let cook a few minutes. Splash in the wine or chicken broth. Reduce slightly, then transfer the pan to a preheated 350-degree oven and bake for about 20 minutes to finish cooking.

Meanwhile, pour the remaining 2 teaspoons of oil into a small wok or skillet, and heat. When the oil is almost smoking, toss in the bell pepper strips and stir-fry rapidly, about a minute, then add the mushrooms and broccoli and stir-fry rapidly again. Add a little water, and let steam cook, covered, until just cooked *al dente*. Now I remove to Mahon's bowl about one-third of the contents of this pan and bone the chicken pieces, giving him as much chicken as I plan to share with him. I season the remaining vegetables and chicken to my liking, and scatter some herbs on top.

# Stir-Fry of Chicken and Seasonal Vegetables

There's nothing like a really good stir-fry, carefully done so that the vegetables are quickly cooked—which brings out their color and crunch—and the meats are meltingly tender and spicy. The secret is not only the fast cooking over high heat, but the addition of just the right touch of marinade and the finishing sauce. It takes practice to master the art, and I always seize the moment to try my hand, guided by the incomparable Chinese cookbook author Irene Kuo, who described the technique with such colorful language that whenever I have the right combination of ingredients to inspire me, I happily get to work. There is always a sense of excitement in the kitchen when you are working at such high speed. In fact, more than once I have set off the fire alarms in our apartment building as the smoke has drifted out into the back hall and I have to call down the stairway—"It's okay, it's only me cooking a Chinese dinner." Little dogs—at least the ones I have known—seem to sense the excitement and want to pitch in. So I have finally worked out a canine-simplified version that reduces some of the garlicky, gingery, salty elements that might not be good for a dog.

**FOR THE MARINADE**

Pinch of salt
1 teaspoon dry sherry
1 teaspoon egg white

1 teaspoon cornstarch
1 teaspoon oil


1 piece chicken breast, about
  5 ounces
1 tablespoon oil
1 large garlic clove, smashed and
  peeled (optional)
7 quarter-sized pieces fresh
  ginger, peeled
½ cup broccoli florets

½ large bell pepper, cut into logs
  similar to the chicken
½ smallish zucchini, cut into
  approximately the same
  shape as the chicken
2 scallions, 1½ to 3 inches long
2 to 3 medium-sized mushrooms,
  sliced
¼ cup or more chicken broth

| | |
|---|---|
| 1 teaspoon soy sauce | 2 or 3 grindings of pepper mill |
| 1 teaspoon oyster sauce | using white pepper |
| 1 teaspoon dry sherry | 1 teaspoon cornstarch dissolved |
| Pinch of salt | in 1 tablespoon water |

Mix all the ingredients for the velvety marinade together in a small bowl, beating gently with a fork just enough to incorporate the egg white but not enough to make it fluffy. Cut the chicken breast in as uniform-sized pieces as you can manage, approximately 1½ inches long and ¼ inch thick. Drop them into the bowl with the marinade and mix with your fingers to coat thoroughly. Cover and refrigerate for at least half an hour. Test before you are ready to stir-fry. Bring 2 quarts of water to a boil and drop the coated chicken pieces in, turn down the heat, and cook gently, stirring a bit to separate the chicken pieces.

Now you're ready to do the stir-fry, so line up the ingredients close to the stove.

Heat the tablespoon of oil in a wok or frying pan and drop the garlic and ginger in. When the oil is sizzling hot, toss in the chicken, broccoli, bell pepper, zucchini, scallions, and mushrooms and toss them together over medium-high heat for about 2 minutes, then semi-cover and turn down the heat and let steam just a minute. Now mix together the sauce ingredients, give them a final whisk, add the chicken broth, and you're all set. Serve with rice.

Once you feel comfortable with stir-frying, all the above will go quickly and you'll find yourself whipping up a stir-fry for you and your dog using other meats or poultry—even shrimp if he likes that. It is the perfect way to get the right balance of proteins, starches, and vegetables all in one bowl, and you can vary the fresh vegetables according to what's in season.

# Chicken, Noodle, and Vegetable Salad

Salads using yesterday's cooked chicken or fish or meat offer lots of possibilities to share with Mabon. I don't mean flimsy salads of baby greens and a sharp vinegary dressing, but substantial bowls of equal parts of vegetables and starch along with the meat protein. This one, with an Asian flavor, offers lots of possibilities for variations, according to the season and what's in the fridge. The dressing is worth having at hand, so I am calling for more than you need for this recipe.

### DRESSING

½ teaspoon dry mustard
1½ teaspoons sugar
1½ teaspoons toasted sesame oil
¼ cup vegetable oil

3 tablespoons white wine vinegar

1½ cups shredded cooked
    chicken

### TOSS-INS

1–1½ ounces fettuccine or Asian
    noodles
About a dozen green beans,
    trimmed
About a dozen snow peas,
    trimmed
2 scallions, including tender
    green parts, trimmed and

sliced, or ½ of a fat shallot,
    peeled and finely chopped
½ small avocado, peeled and
    sliced
1 tablespoon chopped fresh
    cilantro leaves

Put all the dressing ingredients in a bottle, and shake well. Pour a little of this dressing over the chicken, and toss. Chill and let macerate while you prepare the other ingredients.

To cook the toss-ins: Bring a large pot of water to the boil, and stir in the noodles. Let cook 5 minutes, then add the beans, and, after another 3 minutes, add the snow peas and scallions for a final minute of cooking. Fish out a noodle and taste it to make sure it is done *al dente*. Drain the

noodles and vegetables, toss into a strainer, and run cold water over them to cool. Now toss everything, including the avocado, together with the chicken and as much of the dressing as you like (taste is the only measure). Serve yourself a generous helping with cilantro scattered on top. For Mabon, a brimming cupful of this salad would make a fine supper. Just a taste of the dressing would be enough for him, but skip the scallions and cilantro.

Seasonal variations might include shaved
fennel, chopped asparagus, peas, and
sliced baby zucchini.

# Chicken Breast with Winter Squash, Fennel, and Hazelnuts

Here is a delicious way of using the chicken breast and eating some of the vegetables I have roasted for Mabon.

1 tablespoon light olive oil
1 whole boneless chicken breast, trimmed of skin and fat and cut in half

Salt and freshly ground pepper
Splash of white wine and/or chicken broth
2 tablespoons chopped hazelnuts

**FROM THE ROASTING TRAY (SEE PAGE 134)**

3 chunks roasted winter squash, such as butternut (see technique in recipe on page 143)

2 slices roasted fennel (see page 136)
2 to 3 strips roasted red bell pepper (see page 136)

Heat the olive oil, and sauté the chicken pieces, turning them often, until they have browned on both sides, about 10 minutes. Remove the chicken to a shallow baking dish, salt and pepper lightly, strew the roasted vegetables on top, drizzle the white wine and/or chicken broth over all, and sprinkle the hazelnuts on top. Bake in a preheated 350-degree oven for 25 minutes.

If the chicken breast is quite thick,
slice it in half horizontally.

# Chicken Soup

Every good cook should have some homemade chicken soup stashed away in the fridge or the freezer. It's not so hard, particularly if you get a whole chicken now and then. If what you've thrown together seems thin or weak in flavor, buy a package of chicken wings, have a few of them grilled for supper, and throw the rest into the soup pot. Though it would be dangerous to give Mabon a whole bony wing, I might fish a few out of the soup pot after they've cooked through and scrape the cooked meat into his supper dish. As to the chicken soup we're making here, I use not only the carcass and trimmings and small bones, but also scraps I may have saved (see page 37) that are compatible with the chickeny flavor.

Here's a simple formula you can build on.

Use a pot that will hold about 4 quarts. Dump into the soup pot the carcass and stripped down bones, along with 1 onion (including the peel), 1 large carrot, 1 celery stalk, and a handful of parsley. Cover with cold water by 2 inches, add ½ teaspoon salt, and bring to a boil. Skim off the scum, lower the heat, cover, and cook at a lively simmer. For a thin broth, an hour of cooking should be enough. To reduce further and intensify the flavor, cook as much as 1 hour more. I do the final seasoning at the end, remembering to hold back on the salt for Mabon. Some hot chicken soup is a lovely way to warm up his dinner.

# Chicken and Asparagus Gratin

This is an easy dish to make if you have some cooked chicken and dried mushrooms, as well as a few seasonal vegetables. I like to make it in spring, when fresh asparagus is in the markets. As to the cream sauce, I try to keep some in the freezer, so making the gratin is more like an assembly job.

¼ cup dried porcini, soaked in warm water to cover

About 6 asparagus spears, tough ends discarded

½ cup cream sauce or béchamel (see page 43)

About 6 slices of cooked chicken breast, to cover the bottom of a single gratin dish

Salt and freshly ground pepper to taste

1 tablespoon chopped fresh herbs, such as tarragon, young marjoram, and/or parsley and chives

Splash of Madeira (optional)

While the porcini are soaking, cook the asparagus in a medium pot of boiling salted water for 2 minutes. Drain the asparagus spears, and run cold water over them. Drain the porcini and set aside. Heat up the cream sauce, stirring with a whisk (or make it from scratch). Lay the chicken pieces and the porcini on top of the asparagus, and spoon the cream sauce on top, spreading it out to cover the surface. Add salt and pepper. Sprinkle the fresh herbs on top, add the Madeira, if desired, and bake in a pre-heated 350-degree oven for 20 minutes.

In the spring, blanched fiddleheads or artichoke hearts are good; in midsummer, you might try cauliflower or broccoli florets.

# Roast Cornish Game Hen

I like to roast one of these birds whole and find ways of sharing every last morsel with Mabon. An herbal rub with garlic paste is well worth the extra effort to give this small bird a good flavor while roasting. You can vary the herb according to what you may find in the farmers' market or perhaps grow on your windowsill. Tarragon, rosemary, young marjoram leaves, and Italian parsley are all good, and the bit of lemon peel gives a nice zest.

THE HERB RUB

About 2 teaspoons chopped
  fresh rosemary
2 teaspoons chopped fresh
  Italian parsley
1 fat garlic clove, smashed and
  peeled

½ teaspoon salt
Several grinds of black pepper
1 tablespoon olive oil
1 tablespoon chopped lemon peel

1 Cornish game hen

At least ½ hour before roasting (or even the night before), mix together the ingredients for the rub (save a little of the oil to moisten the skin). Loosen the skin around the cavity of the bird, and with your fingers push the rub ingredients beneath the skin into the breast and thighs. Pat the skin with the reserved oil and roast the bird in a shallow pan in a 375-degree oven, breast side down, for 20 minutes. Then turn the bird breast side up and roast another 15–20 minutes, or until the juices run clear. If you want to roast some vegetables alongside, see pages 135–138 for ideas. I always allow some for Mabon. He also gets the prize gizzard and heart, and I get the liver. Just toss these treasures into the roasting pan for about the final 5 or 6 minutes of cooking.

# Ground Turkey "Pâté"

The frozen ground turkey that I got for Mabon needed to be eaten up. But how to make this bland meat look and taste appealing? Then I thought of the slices of *pâté de campagne* that we used to get from neighborhood charcuteries all over Paris, and I decided to try to emulate that, using a mini–loaf pan. So I borrowed the turkey from Mabon, and those who tasted my creation seemed quite pleased with it.

⅓ cup fresh breadcrumbs
½ cup milk
1½ cups ground turkey
½ beaten egg (see page 79)
Salt and freshly ground pepper
Pinch of curry powder

Pinch of turmeric
2 teaspoons crushed dried
    mushrooms
1 teaspoon grated fresh ginger
Butter, for greasing the pan

Soak the breadcrumbs in the milk, and when they're moistened, squeeze out the liquid and discard it. Add to the breadcrumbs the ground turkey, egg, salt and pepper to taste, and a pinch of curry and turmeric. Add the dried mushrooms crumbled into small pieces, and freshly grated ginger. Mix well with your hands to work in the seasonings. Butter generously a mini–meatloaf or bread pan, and turn the "pâté" ingredients into the pan. Bake it in a preheated 350-degree oven for 40 minutes, and then let cool at least 10 minutes before unmolding. This is good warm, as a supper dish or as a snack with a glass of wine. Sorry, Mabon, you're not invited for the latter (even in France).

# Turkey Burgers

Another good use for Mabon's large package of ground turkey is to make a simple but tasty turkey burger for myself, or one for each of us, keeping his burger unseasoned and simple.

About ¼ pound ground turkey
1 scallion, including tender green parts, trimmed and finely chopped
3 or 4 sprigs of fresh Italian parsley, chopped
¼ teaspoon curry powder
Salt and freshly ground pepper to taste

½ teaspoon grated fresh ginger
1 tablespoon olive oil
Splash of beef broth or red wine
A dollop of Dijon mustard
Hamburger bun or equal-sized baguette, split in half horizontally

Mix together all ingredients through the grated ginger in a bowl with your hands. Form into a hamburger-sized patty.

Heat the oil in a small pan, slip the patty in, and brown on both sides; then turn down the heat a little, and cook about 1 minute on each side. Test to see if the meat is still uncooked inside; if so, cook a little longer. Do not press the patty with a spatula, because that will release all the juices and give you a dry hamburger. Remove to a warm plate. Splash a little beef broth or wine into the pan, and let sizzle. Pour the *jus* over the burger. Smear a dollop of mustard on top of the burger, and enjoy on the bread of your choice. I use just a little mustard on Mabon's portion (without any bread); he seems to like it.

# Eggs

What a godsend the chicken's eggs can be in everyday cooking—especially when an unexpected guest shows up for lunch, or when I have let Mabon's meat run out. Either an omelet or a frittata can do the trick, dressed up with tasty garnishes I've tucked away. Add a little starch component and you have a satisfying, well-balanced meal for yourself and one hungry pup.

## Measuring Eggs

A recipe that calls for a teaspoon of egg might puzzle the inexperienced cook. But it's a perfectly reasonable amount to use, particularly when you are reducing a recipe. And it's not hard to obtain. One tablespoon of raw egg equals three teaspoons. So, if you want one teaspoon, simply crack the egg into a small jar with a tight-fitting lid and shake it up until the white and yolk are well blended. Using a one-teaspoon measuring spoon, dip into the egg and extract that amount. Refrigerate what is left. After a few days, you can scramble the leftover egg and toss it into your dog's supper. *Waste not, want not.*

P.S. I have only recently learned that in your local supermarket you can buy cartons of egg whites and of egg yolks, ready to use.

# A Shirred Egg

A shirred egg is cooked under the broiler in a very small frying pan or an ovenproof shallow baking dish. There is usually something tasty tucked in, such as a chicken liver, but in these days of mass-produced poultry, such treasures seem to be disappearing. If there is a gizzard and heart, Mabon gets them.

2 teaspoons unsalted butter
1 medium-sized shallot, peeled
    and chopped
1 chicken liver

Splash of sherry
1 large egg
Salt and freshly ground
    pepper

Melt 1 teaspoon of the butter in your small pan or dish, add the shallot and the liver and fry for 2–3 minutes over medium heat, turning several times. Add a splash of sherry, and cook down to a glaze. Break the egg into the center of the pan, salt and pepper everything, and slip the pan under a preheated broiler—about 6 inches from the heat. Cook about 1 minute, basting 2 to 3 times with the remaining butter. I prepare Mabon's share the same way, using a small egg and skipping the sherry and shallot.

Note: If you can't get that single chicken liver,
try using a piece of sausage or a slice of calves'
liver, cut off from a big piece.

# A Steamed Egg
# Nestled in Brussels Sprouts

Of course, you can nestle an egg in a variety of vegetables—one dish for you, and a smaller one for your dog. Perhaps he would like it if you dropped in a few slivers of cooked meat, to make a well-rounded meal.

6 or 7 medium-sized Brussels
  sprouts
2 teaspoons light olive oil or
  vegetable oil
Salt and freshly ground pepper
  to taste

1 egg
A few small pieces of creamy
  semi-soft cheese
A heaping tablespoon of aged
  grating cheese

Trim the root ends from the Brussels sprouts. Tear off the tough outer leaves, and cut each sprout in half. Pour the oil into a sauté pan just large enough to accommodate the sprouts, then slip the sprouts into the pan. Turn once, salt and pepper to taste, and set over medium heat. Brown lightly, then add enough water to come halfway up the sprouts. Cook about 2 minutes. Crack the egg into the center of the pan. Cover, and cook about 3 minutes. Taste, and, if almost done, tuck in the nibbles of soft cheese and sprinkle the grated cheese on top. Return the pan to low heat until the cheeses melt.

# An Omelet to Share

For an omelet that I am going to share with Mabon, I use three eggs and a 9-inch pan. Then, when the omelet is done, I lop off a third of it for his bowl. You can experiment with amounts. Omelets are very flexible.

| | |
|---|---|
| 2 teaspoons unsalted butter | About ¼ cup filling at room |
| 3 large eggs | temperature or warm (see |
| Salt and freshly ground pepper | page 84 for suggestions) |

While you heat the butter in a 9-inch nonstick pan over medium heat, quickly crack the eggs into a bowl. Season them with just a little salt and pepper (you'll be adding more to your share when the omelet is done), and beat with a fork until the whites and yolks are just blended. The butter in the pan should be hot and sizzling by now, and when the large bubbles start to subside, pour the eggs in and let them set for just 10 seconds. With the flat side of your fork against the bottom of the pan, vigorously move the mass of eggs all around. Let them set again for just a few seconds, and then, with the tines of the fork, pull the parts of the eggs that have set around the rim toward the center, and tilt the pan slightly so that the uncooked liquidy parts flow onto the bare spots and set. This whole process should take about 1 minute. Now spoon the filling across the center of the eggs, and give the pan a very firm jerk or two so that the egg mass at the far edge of the pan flips forward onto the filling (you can nudge it with a spatula if it needs help). Turn the omelet out onto a warm plate, letting the filled part settle on the plate first, and then tilt the pan further and flip the remaining, uncovered part over the top. And, voilà, you have a perfect omelet. If it isn't quite perfect, *tant pis.*

*After I arrange this omelet on a plate for me,*
*I'll cut off about a third for*
*Mabon's supper.*

# Ideas for Omelet Fillings

- Cooked vegetables cut into small pieces are always good, particularly roasted vegetables.

- Cheeses add a special zest, either grated or cut into small chunks.

- Meaty accents always appeal to Mabon. Try a little shredded ham or prosciutto, cooked crumbled sausage, roughly chopped and cooked chicken livers, or yesterday's meal of chicken or turkey.

- Fishy accents appeal to Mabon, too. Bland fish is disappointing, but smoked fish—salmon, trout, finnan haddie—are all good with eggs. Leftover fresh salmon or any flaky, tasty fish will do as well.

# Have I Created a Monster?

*Taffy was a Welshman,*
*Taffy was a thief;*
*Taffy came to my house*
*And stole a piece of beef . . .*

I can't get those lines out of my head as I look once again at that self-satisfied expression on Mabon's face, his long tongue protruding to lick up the last scraps of whatever he has just filched from the supper table when I let down my guard. Even before I check, I know. It isn't a piece of beef but a generous slab of that Gorgonzola dolce that I just put on the cheese platter and was hoping to enjoy for dessert. Yesterday it was half of a ham-and-cheese sandwich that he made away with, and he has already defied, twice, the rule that chocolate can kill a dog.

Is it because I have developed in him such a highly refined palate that it is natural for him to go after good food, even though he knows it is not good for him? Or is it that the smell of my cooking is so intoxicating that he can't help himself?

Smell—undoubtedly, that is the key, and, like all highly developed senses, it can serve a creature well or destructively. I am reminded of a time in Vermont, about a dozen years ago, when Mabon's predecessor came to live with my husband and me. He had grown up on a farm where he had been mistreated, and was finally sent to a shelter. We fell in love with him and took him home on the condition that he must be nice to our Welsh terrier Teg, who had become senile and

*Madoc*

was finding it hard to navigate her last days on earth. Madoc seemed to understand and was gentle and loving with her.

One day, we thought we had lost Teg when she had wandered off, and then we spotted her at the distant pond, walking around and around, not knowing where she was. "Go get her," we cried to Madoc, and he knew immediately what we wanted. He raised his head, sniffed the air for direction, and took off at a fast, sure run. When they met, Teg wagged her tail, and they walked slowly back up the hill.

Madoc's sure sense of smell didn't always serve him well, however. It seems that he would forever associate the smell of manure with those bullying farm boys, and he took it out on my cousin and his son. He would attack their manure-smelling boots so ferociously that he bit through one and into the flesh of my cousin John Reynolds, of all people. John is the man who tends our cattle and herds them lovingly from pasture to pasture.

It is all a lesson in the power of smell, and I must remember, dogs will be dogs. Taffy will always go for the beef, and Mabon will jump high onto any table for a hunk of that Gorgonzola. And I must be forgiving—which, of course, I am.

# A Frittata

I'll often make a frittata for lunch, particularly when I have just a few strips of sweet pepper or a couple of ready-to-use-up scallions, or a bit of a left-over cooked vegetable in the fridge, such as zucchini, fennel, asparagus, a small potato—you name it. Anything goes. Lately, I have been making a larger, three-egg frittata so that I can give a third of it to Mabon. He can't wait to put his nose into the warm eggs. In fact, the other day he didn't bother to wait. When I left my frittata on the table to go answer the phone, he climbed quickly into my chair and had devoured half of it before I caught him in the act.

2 tablespoons olive oil
2 scallions, including tender green parts, trimmed and cut into 4 strips each
About 4 strips bell pepper
6 strips ham or cooked sausage
A small handful of cooked vegetables (see suggestions above)
1 small cooked potato, sliced
3 large eggs
Salt and freshly ground pepper
2 heaping tablespoons grated cheese

Heat the olive oil in an 8- or 9-inch omelet pan and cook the scallions and bell pepper a couple of minutes, until they soften a little. Strew the strips of meat and the other vegetables over the bottom of the pan—in a pattern if you like. Beat the eggs lightly, and season them, as well as the vegetables in the pan, with salt and pepper to taste. Turn the heat to very low, then pour the eggs into the pan, shaking it to distribute them evenly. Cover, and cook very slowly over low heat. Check often. When the liquid begins to solidify, remove the pan from the heat and sprinkle the cheese all over the top. Now slip the pan about 2 inches under a preheated broiler and brown the surface lightly. Let cool a bit, and cut in wedges.

When you dish up, avoid the bell pepper and scallions in the canine portion.

# Fish

We know now how very good it is to have fish in our diet, and that applies to our dogs' diet as well. It can be expensive, but a little dog does not need much to make a difference. I try to look for less-expensive fish, such as talapia, and I invariably have something left over for a salad, a hash, a fishcake, or a gratin, or in fried rice or pasta. I also look for varieties that don't have too many small bones. Sardines have been singled out as being particularly healthy for dogs, but don't try to fish out their tiny bones yourself. Instead, use good canned sardines. In fact, always keep a few cans in the cupboard, to fall back on for your dog's dinner when you have run out of the protein quota for his supper—it's much better than opening a can of commercial dog food.

# Whole Fish Roasted

I love to buy a whole fish, to roast or steam. For one thing, you can tell if the fish is really fresh, which you can't do once it is filleted. The eyes should be bright and clear, the skin shiny, and it should smell good. Trout, snapper, small bass, and branzino are good choices, and you can judge those qualities only when you see the fish whole. A fish of about 1–1¼ pounds is usually the right size for me, with a good portion for Mabon.

1 whole fish, about 1–1¼ pounds
Light olive oil or vegetable oil
Salt and freshly ground pepper
6–8 thin slivers of fennel bulb
2 scallions, including tender green parts, trimmed and cut into thin slivers
3 quarter-sized slices of fresh ginger, peeled and slivered
2 or 3 small mushrooms, finely chopped (optional)
1 small garlic clove, peeled and slivered
Lemon wedges
2 tablespoons chopped fresh cilantro or parsley

Have the fish cleaned and gutted, but leave bones in and the head on. Make three slashes on each side, rub in a little oil, and salt and pepper lightly all over. Set the fish on an ovenproof platter, insert some of the fennel, scallions, ginger, and mushrooms into the cavity, and strew remaining pieces around the fish. Insert the garlic slivers into the slashes. Roast in a preheated 375-degree oven for 20 minutes, or until the flesh of the fish is easily pierced and can be lifted from the bone. I have my portion with steamed potatoes and the roasting vegetables, along with lemon wedges, and sprinkle the cilantro on top.

I manage to extract a good serving for Mabon by running my fingers against the bones and easing out the meat from around the neck and tail, then adding some of the fillet to make a 3 ounce portion. Be very careful to get out all the tiny bones and dispose of them in a safe place. Embellish your dog's portion with a vegetable he likes and a starch.

# Broiled Haddock, Bluefish, or Mackerel over a Bed of Fennel and Potatoes

2 teaspoons light olive oil or vegetable oil
1 bluefish or mackerel fillet, about 1¼ pounds
1 fat shallot, peeled and sliced
1 medium-sized new potato, sliced
½ fennel bulb, trimmed of tough exterior and sliced
¼ cup heavy cream
Salt and freshly ground pepper to taste

Heat the oil in a skillet just big enough to accommodate the fish fillet, or cut the fish into two pieces. Toss in the shallot, potato slices, and fennel, and sauté for about 5 minutes. When the incidental liquid is almost absorbed, pour the cream into the pan, scraping up any browned bits. Lay the fish on top, and season with salt and pepper. Set the skillet 3 inches under a preheated broiler and broil about 7 minutes. What Mabon and I don't eat goes into a salad the next day.

# Monkfish with Summer Vegetables

Here is another good fish for dogs. Because what we eat of the monkfish is solid meat, you don't have to painstakingly bone it. This fish used to be considered trash fish, maybe because it was so ugly. But it is now honored among most cooks as a subtle-tasting delicacy that absorbs the aromatic seasonings it is cooked in.

2 tablespoons light olive oil or vegetable oil

1 fat shallot, peeled and thinly sliced

1 medium-sized tomato, peeled, seeded, and chopped

½ sweet red bell pepper, seeded and sliced

1 garlic clove, peeled and finely sliced

Salt and freshly ground pepper to taste

Splash of white wine

About 1¼ pounds monkfish

1 small zucchini, sliced

2 scallions, including tender green parts, trimmed and cut into 1-inch pieces

About 2 tablespoons chopped fresh herbs, such as basil, tarragon, and/or parsley

Heat the oil in a medium sauté pan, sauté the shallot 1 minute, then add the chopped tomato, bell pepper slices, and garlic. Salt and pepper to taste. Cook until the juices are released. Pour in the wine, and bring to a boil. Push aside the vegetables, and drop the monkfish into the pan. Turn the fish until all sides become golden. Then smother with the vegetables, cover, reduce the heat, and simmer for 15 minutes. Add the zucchini slices and scallions, cover, and simmer another 4–5 minutes. The fish should be tender; to test, pierce with a fork. Sprinkle the herbs on top.

What Mabon and I don't consume on the first round goes into a salad for me, and there is usually still a piece to add to Mabon's protein portion for tomorrow's supper.

# Panfried Catfish Fillet

Catfish made the front page of *The New York Times* recently as one of the fish we should be eating, rich as it is in omega-3. So, following my instinct that what's good for me is usually good for Mabon (unless I'm told otherwise), I brought home a fillet weighing about ¾ pound and fried it in butter and oil after coating it first in the Japanese crumb mixture panko (you can use fresh breadcrumbs, but it won't be quite as tasty or crunchy). Mabon liked his share and even finished off the fennel that I served with it.

Salt and freshly ground pepper
1 catfish fillet, cut into 2 pieces,
    Mabon's about 3 ounces, mine
    about 6 or 7 ounces
1 tablespoon unsalted butter

1 tablespoon light olive oil or
    vegetable oil
About ½ cup panko bread-
    crumbs
Lemon wedge (for me)

Rub a little salt and freshly ground pepper into the larger piece of catfish, leaving the smaller piece unseasoned. Heat the butter and oil in a smallish frying pan that will just accommodate the catfish pieces. Dredge the fillets in the panko, patting them firmly on both sides, then slip the fish into the pan. Cook over moderate heat about 3 minutes each side—maybe 4 for the thicker piece—turning once or twice. The fish has to cook through, so don't brown too quickly. I like a few squeezes of lemon on my fish, but not for Mabon. Good with a side dish that combines a vegetable and a starch.

"I love New York, too."

# Broiled or Grilled Salmon

Salmon is one of the most reliably available fish one can find, and it is full of good nutrients. I like to spice my portion up a bit, and have put into practice some good tricks I have learned from Madhur Jaffrey, the wonderful Indian cookbook author, about giving the flesh a rub with a few spices before cooking. I like the fillet, and I leave the skin on to keep the fish moist. But I'm told the fatty skin is too rich for dogs. Too bad!

⅛ teaspoon turmeric
Pinch of salt
Several grindings of black pepper

Pinch of cayenne pepper
1 salmon fillet, about 1¼ pounds

OPTIONAL

3 tablespoons Dijon mustard
A couple of squeezes of lemon
    juice

1 tablespoon chopped fresh
    cilantro

At least ½ hour before cooking, mix together in a bowl the turmeric, salt, black pepper, and cayenne. Rub this mix all over the flesh side of the salmon, cover lightly, and let stand for at least 30 minutes at room temperature. If you are macerating the fish any longer, wrap the fillet and refrigerate for 2 to 3 hours. Preheat the broiler (or grill). Set the salmon, skin side down, on a lightly oiled baking sheet, and broil 5–6 minutes, or until done to your liking. If it seems uncooked in the middle, turn off the broiler and let finish cooking in a 350-degree oven for 3 or 4 minutes or more. If you have used the grill, remove from the direct heat and cover for the time needed to finish cooking. For a spicier version, smear the Dijon mustard, lemon juice, and cilantro together on top of the fillet, then put it back under the broiler for less than a minute.

Despite the spiciness, Mabon gobbled up his portion and looked for more.

# Salmon Cakes

Here is a satisfying way to use up some cooked salmon or other fish. If you don't happen to have a leftover cooked potato in your fridge, put a potato in a small pot of water to boil; it should be done in about 20 minutes. Peel and mash with a little butter and cream.

1 cup flaked cooked salmon
1 medium potato, cooked and
    mashed with butter and cream
2 or 3 scallions, including tender
    green parts, trimmed and
    finely chopped
1 teaspoon grated fresh ginger
Salt and freshly ground pepper
    to taste

About 1 tablespoon chopped
    fresh basil or tarragon, or
    ¼ teaspoon dried
1 tablespoon beaten egg (see
    page 79)
About ½ cup panko breadcrumbs
1 tablespoon light olive oil or
    vegetable oil

Mix together the fish, potato, scallions, and seasonings. Form the mixture into three cakes. Brush both sides of the cakes with the beaten egg, and then dredge in the panko breadcrumbs. Heat the oil in a medium skillet, and gently fry the salmon cakes about 3 minutes on each side.

# Starches: Rice, Grains, Dried Beans, Pasta

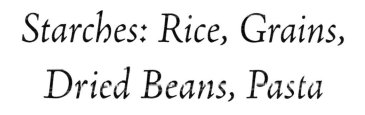

"Starches" does not sound like a particularly seductive category, but the foods that it encompasses—rice (white, brown, and all the varieties), grains, grits, polenta, dried beans, and pastas—offer many delights that most dogs appreciate. Just remember to keep the proportion of starch to one-third or less of the total supper. Many of the dishes I offer here can be done ahead of time, so that the rice or the surprisingly tasty other grains, such as quinoa and farro, can just be warmed and dressed up quickly for your impatient companion.

# Rice

Here are the rices I have used most for cooking since Mabon came into my life.

- Long-grain California rice. Pour 1 cup of rice into 2 cups of water, and bring to a lively simmer. Cover, and cook for 15 minutes. Let stand for 5 minutes, covered, and then fluff up with a fork. Add salt and pepper if you wish.

- Brown rice—not as refined as white rice, and therefore healthier for your dog. You'll need 45–50 minutes for cooking, and at least three times more water than rice in volume.

- I use short-grain rice mostly for making risottos.

- Basmati I usually reserve for Indian dishes, but it is so delicious I sometimes make it plain for Mabon and me. Be sure to rinse it several times just before cooking.

# Brown Rice

Brown rice is highly recommended for dogs, so I tend to prepare it quite often, putting away what's left over to round out future dinners for Mabon. It's particularly good with a mix of roasted vegetables.

1 cup brown rice
3–4 cups water

2 teaspoons unsalted butter (optional)
Pinch of salt (optional)

Put rice and 3 cups of water in a small heavy pot, and bring to a boil. Lower the heat, cover, and boil gently, checking the water level once or twice and adding more water if necessary. Cook about 45 minutes, then taste. All the water should be absorbed, and the rice should be tender; if not, cook longer. When the rice is done to your liking, turn off the heat and let steep 5 minutes, covered, then fluff up with a fork. If desired, season your portion with a little butter and salt.

# A Casserole of Rice and Vegetables

This recipe uses cooked rice, so plan ahead. You can vary it by using differ-ent greens and adding tidbits of other seasonal vegetables you may have on hand. Even Mabon seems to forget his prejudice against those bitter leaves when they are surrounded by good eats.

2 handfuls of leafy green
   vegetables (spinach, Swiss
   chard, young beet greens,
   turnip greens)
1 tablespoon olive oil
1 garlic clove, peeled and
   slivered
¾ cup grated zucchini (optional)

1 cup cooked rice, brown if you
   prefer
4 teaspoons butter
Salt and freshly ground pepper
   to taste
About ¼ cup fresh breadcrumbs
A generous sprinkling of good
   aged grated cheese

Rinse the greens, and cut off the stems (they can go into scrap soup; see page 37). Heat the olive oil in a small wok or skillet, and fry the garlic lightly; then dump in the greens and stir them around. Add the optional grated zucchini and a little water, and cook for about 3 minutes. Toss in the rice and half the butter. Add a little salt and pepper to taste. Trans-fer to a shallow casserole, cover lightly with breadcrumbs, dot with the remaining butter, and sprinkle on as much cheese as you like all over the top. If you have used long-grain white rice, bake in a preheated 350-degree oven for about 25 minutes. Brown rice could use an additional 5–10 min-utes of baking.

# Wild Rice

Wild rice is really a grain, not a rice, and the best of it comes from the upper Midwest, where Native Americans still harvest the rice by beating the ripened grains into their canoes. We have always ordered directly from Blackduck, Minnesota—the company is now called Slindee Wild Rice. Wild rice not only tastes good, but it packs a lot of nourishment. Embellished with an assortment of colorful vegetables, it makes a meal, although Mabon would prefer to have a little leftover meat tucked in. If you use the cultivated variety, adjust the cooking time; it usually takes about 40 minutes. So, as always, taste to be sure it is done to your liking.

# Wild Rice Pilaf

If you are using cultivated wild rice, it will take less time than traditional wild rice.

⅔ cup wild rice
3 cups water
A large pinch of salt
2 tablespoons butter
4 or 5 medium-sized mushrooms
About 8 snow peas, blanched

3 scallions, including tender green parts, trimmed
A scattering of slivered almonds
2 or 3 strips country ham (optional)

Rinse the rice in running water, rubbing it through your fingers. Drain, and put in a small heavy pot with 2½ cups of cold water and a pinch of salt. Bring to a boil, then turn down the heat. Cover, and cook at a lively simmer for 50 minutes, checking to see if it needs more water. Taste, and if the rice is tender (but still a bit chewy) and the water is absorbed, it's done; otherwise, cook for another 5 minutes, adding a little more water if needed. In a separate pan, melt the butter and sauté the mushrooms. When they're almost tender, toss in the snow peas and scallions and cook for another 2–3 minutes. When you're ready to eat, make a mound of wild rice and garnish with the mushrooms, snow peas, scallions, almonds, and if you like, ham. The almonds are not so good for some little dogs, so don't embellish those portions.

*Young Teg on her hilltop*

# Wild Mushroom Risotto

Nora Kim and Les Hook, the wild-food specialists of northern Vermont, wrote so appreciatively of the distinctive flavor of their dried pheasant-back mushrooms that I decided I had to try a risotto for Mabon and me using Nora's sample package of these gifts of the woods. Nora recommended a way of rehydrating them in cream that appealed to me (be sure to save the soaking cream to fold in to the rice for a final flourish). You can, of course, use other dried mushrooms.

¼ cup heavy cream
⅔ ounce (1 package) dried pheasant-back mushrooms or other dried mushrooms
1 tablespoon butter
1 fat shallot, peeled and finely chopped
¾ cup short-grain risotto rice, such as Arborio

¼ cup white wine
2 cups hot chicken broth
Salt and freshly ground pepper to taste
A scattering of chopped fresh herbs (parsley, chives, tarragon, if available)
Grated Parmesan cheese to taste

About ½ hour before cooking, heat the cream. Put the mushrooms in a bowl, and pour the cream over them. Set aside in a warm place, and let steep 30 minutes. Now start your risotto. Heat the butter in a small to medium heavy saucepan, and when it's sizzling, toss in the shallot, rice, and mushrooms (saving the cream). Stir them as you add the wine and about a third of the chicken broth, taking care to scrape the rice from the bottom of the pan. When the liquid has been absorbed, add another third of the broth, and the final third along with the reserved cream. All of this should take about 15–20 minutes. Taste carefully now, add salt and pepper to taste, then fold in the herbs and cheese.

# Grits with Shrimp

Here is a simple dinner that I enjoy making when Mabon's stock of cooked grains is running low. I do the final seasoning after scooping out his portion (about a quarter of the amount of grits called for here). Good stone-ground grits make all the difference, so get them if you can. And you can substitute okra for the broccoli if you like okra, or try asparagus if it's in season.

1 cup milk
1 cup water, or more as needed
½ cup stone-ground grits, soaked, rinsed, then drained
2 teaspoons light cooking oil
1 tablespoon butter
1 fat garlic clove, peeled and slivered
¾ cup broccoli florets
¼ red or orange bell pepper, cut into narrow 2-inch-long strips

6–8 ounces medium-sized shrimp, peeled, or a few more if your dog likes shrimp
Salt and freshly ground pepper
A generous splash of white wine
1 scallion, including tender green parts, finely chopped
Fresh parsley or another herb (optional)

Bring the milk and water to a boil in a medium-sized saucepan. Pour in the grits, stirring, and cook at a simmer for about 45 minutes, continuing to stir frequently and scraping up the grits from the bottom of your cooking pot. If you are not using stone-ground grits, the cooking time will be much shorter, so check after 20 minutes by tasting.

Remove about a quarter of the cooked grits and save for your dog's portion. Heat the oil and butter in a wok or big, heavy pan, and toss in the garlic slivers, broccoli florets, and bell pepper strips. When they are sizzling, scatter in the shrimp. Season with salt and pepper, and stir-fry for 3 or 4 minutes. Pour in a generous splash of white wine, and let it reduce a little. Spoon your portion of grits into a warm bowl, season it with salt and pepper, and then toss in the shrimp, vegetables, and pan juices. If you have some scallion and fresh herbs handy, such as parsley, tarragon, or basil, scatter a small handful, roughly chopped, on top. I withhold the scallion and herbs from Mabon's portion. Any leftover grits can be fried or grilled (Mabon likes the crunch).

*Mabon at work*

## A Job for the Pot Licker

Pans in which you slowly cook grains such as grits, polenta, risotto, and other starches can be hell to clean, so too often the home cook steers away from making a slow-cooked, old-fashioned bowl of grits. It is not because the constant stirring is tiresome; in fact, I always love the gentle, contemplative motion of stirring (and you can tend to another chore now and then, or turn on some music, and stir to the rhythm). But when you are done, you still have that sticky pot to scrape clean. I've tried everything with not much success, and finally I've discovered that my little canine "pot licker" does the best job. It's important to get the pot to him still warm (but not scorching hot); he will tackle it ferociously, thrusting his long tongue into all the crevices. There's still some soaking to be done, but Mabon does all the initial work—and he does a great job.

*Madoc was also a pot licker, but unlike Mabon he couldn't get all four feet into the machine.*

# Baked Polenta

I learned from Marion Cunningham, our twentieth-century Fannie Farmer, how simple it is to prepare cornmeal (or polenta) by baking it with some aromatic vegetables and perhaps an accent of cured meat. It makes a fine dinner as is, and if you want to have extra polenta to grill for another meal, or to fill your dog's quota of grain for his supper, then double the amount of cornmeal called for here and use about 2 cups water.

2 tablespoons light olive oil
1 small onion, chopped
1 medium-sized tomato, seeded and chopped
¾ cup blanched greens (see procedure below), such as spinach, beet greens, chard, or young milkweed leaves

⅓ cup polenta
1 cup warm water
Salt and freshly ground pepper
About 6 strips prosciutto (optional)
3 tablespoons grated Parmesan cheese

Heat 1 tablespoon of the oil, and sauté the onion for a couple of minutes; then add the tomato. Cook and toss the two together for a minute, and stir in the greens, which you have blanched in boiling water for about 1 minute. Now put the polenta in a shallow baking dish, and stir in the warm water and remaining olive oil. Add the sautéed vegetables, salt and pepper lightly, and stir everything together. Bake in a preheated 350-degree oven for 25 minutes. Five minutes before the finish, scatter the prosciutto strips, if using, on top and sprinkle the cheese over all. Return to the oven for a final 5 minutes.

# Lemon-Flavored Quinoa
# with Vegetables

The South American grain quinoa has recently become popular here, particularly among vegetarians. You can understand why when you taste it. Its nutty flavor and slightly chewy texture are satisfying, and it absorbs the flavors of whatever accompaniments you give it.

2 cups water
Salt
1 cup quinoa
Lemon zest from ¼ lemon,
    cut into strips
Juice of ½ small lemon
2 tablespoons olive oil
1 smallish eggplant, some skin
    left on, cut into chunks
1 medium-sized tomato, seeded
    and finely chopped into small
    pieces

¼ red bell pepper, seeded and
    cut into strips
1 small onion, peeled and
    chopped
2 or 3 medium-sized mushrooms
    (optional)
Butter
A sprinkling of chopped fresh
    parsley

Bring the water, lightly salted, to a boil, and sprinkle in the quinoa. Cover the pot, and cook gently for 20 minutes. Stir in the lemon zest and juice, and let steep, off heat, covered. Meanwhile, in the olive oil in a medium-sized heavy frying pan, sauté the eggplant, tomato, bell pepper, onion, and mushrooms, if using, until lightly browned. Turn down the heat, salt to taste, and continue to cook the vegetables until tender. When the quinoa is ready, it should have absorbed all the water; if not, cook a little longer.

Give yourself a generous serving of the quinoa, and stir in a little butter and salt to taste. Surround with the vegetables, and top with a sprinkling of parsley. There will be plenty of quinoa left, so you can tuck it away to serve as the starch portion of another doggy dinner. Mabon doesn't seem to care much for eggplant (he varies on this). But I offer him a taste along with other seasonal vegetables, which you might have yourself with the quinoa, and which seem to please the canine palate—peas, broccoli, and most roasted vegetables (see pages 135–138).

# Farro with Roasted Eggplant
# and Cumin-Scented Yogurt

Farro is another grain that has become recently popular; it provides a healthy, tasty, and substantial kick to your dog's dinner.

### THE SAUCE

½ cup yogurt

½ teaspoon cumin, toasted


¾ cup farro

3 cups water

Butter to taste

Salt

1 medium eggplant

Light olive oil or vegetable oil

¼ red or yellow bell pepper, cut into strips

¾ medium-sized onion, cut into slim rounds

Prepare the sauce first so the flavor of the roasted cumin can permeate the yogurt. Simply stir the two together, and let stand in a warm place. (Leave out the cumin for your dog's portion.) Rinse the farro, rubbing the grain through your fingers. Then strain, and empty into a medium-sized cooking pot. Pour the 3 cups water over, and bring to a boil. Cook at a lively simmer for 20 minutes and taste; the farro should still be a bit chewy but just tender enough. Now drain, and set aside in a warm spot.

Toss your portion with butter and salt to taste. Meanwhile, cut the eggplant into ¾-inch-thick lengthwise slices. Rub olive oil over all the vegetables. Roast in a preheated 400-degree oven for 30 minutes, until the vegetables are softened and just beginning to brown. Arrange the vegetables on top of the farro, and add a dollop of the yogurt sauce—scented for you, plain for your dog.

# Kasha

Kasha is not really a grain. It is the seed of a plant, and it has a long history. Russians love it. It makes a great supper dish for your dog, garnished with a rainbow of seasonal vegetables. I like it as a salad, too, so Mabon lets me borrow from his stash of cooked kasha. Frying the kernels is the secret to making the groats a bit crunchy—and we know that dogs like crunch.

1 cup kasha
1 egg
1 tablespoon vegetable oil

2 cups water
Salt to taste

Rinse the kasha in water, running it through your fingers. Drain through a strainer, shaking it to get rid of the water. Beat the egg in a bowl to blend, and dump the kasha in, stirring well to coat all the kernels. Heat the oil in quite a large pan, and dump in the kasha. Cook, stirring, for 2 or 3 minutes, until the kernels are separated and lightly browned. Pour the 2 cups of water into the pan, salt lightly, and bring to a boil. Lower the heat to a lively simmer, cover, and cook 15 minutes. Give yourself and your little guy generous portions, and strew any roasted vegetables around that you may have handy.

# Green Lentils with Sausage and Mushrooms

Lentils make a nice warming dish that I like to share with Mabon on a chilly Vermont evening. And there will be plenty of unadorned cooked lentils for him, to fulfill his healthy starch quota for days ahead.

1½ cups green lentils
1 small onion, peeled and
   chopped
3 cups water
4 medium-sized cremini
   mushrooms, quartered
Butter

¼ cup beef or chicken
   broth
1 or 2 links of cooked white or
   other mild sausage, cut into
   1-inch pieces
Salt and freshly ground pepper
   to taste

Rinse the lentils, and put them in a medium-sized pot with the onion and water. Bring to a boil, and cook at a lively simmer for about 45 minutes. For a baked dish, for just you and a small dog, sauté the mushrooms in butter until tender and starting to brown. Add a generous cup of drained lentils, the broth, sausage, and salt and pepper to taste. Stir all together, and transfer to a small casserole dish. Bake in a preheated 350-degree oven for about 30 minutes. For Mabon's portion, I scoop up ½ cup of the cooked lentils and, if they are not yet tender, simmer with more water for up to 20 minutes. Mix the lentils into your dog's bowl with a few pieces of sausage meat.

# Red Lentils

Madhur Jaffrey calls these red lentils her "soul food," a staple on her family's table when she was growing up. They adapt very well to Mabon's and my system of sharing, as do many Indian recipes, because the spiciness that is not good for the canine tummy goes in at the last moment and can easily be withheld from Mabon's portion.

1 cup red lentils, washed and dried
¼ teaspoon ground turmeric
1 medium-sized onion, half of it finely chopped, the other half thinly sliced
3 cups water
Salt to taste
3 tablespoons olive oil or canola oil
2 garlic cloves, peeled and thinly sliced
2 or 3 dried hot red chilies, each broken in half

Put the lentils, turmeric, and chopped onion into a medium-sized pan with the water, and bring to a boil. Lower the heat, and cook at a brisk simmer, about 20 minutes, until the lentils are very tender and have absorbed the water. Now remove about a third of the lentils to your pet's bowl. Salt the remaining lentils to your liking. Meanwhile, heat the oil in a small pan, and stir in the sliced onion. Add the garlic and chilies (watch out—these chilies are hot; you may want to use less). Continue to fry and stir until the onion and garlic have turned a golden red. Stir this into the portion of the lentils that you will be eating.

# Lamb with Dried Beans
# (Flageolets or Great Northern)

I have a weakness for the small French dried beans called flageolets, because I first tasted them when I was living in Paris in the late 1940s. I made a lot of bean dishes in those days: they were inexpensive, and wonderfully filling. Great Northern beans are a good substitute.

¾ cup dried beans
1½ cups water
1 medium-sized onion, chopped
Salt to taste
4 smallish mushrooms, cut into small dice
1 garlic clove, peeled and slivered

Several chunks of braised lamb (or cooked beef, or other leftover meat)
About ¼ cup lamb braising liquid or meat broth
Several sprigs of fresh parsley, chopped

Let the beans soak overnight in water to cover. Drain, and put them in a pot with the 1½ cups water and chopped onion. Cook at least 30 minutes, then taste. If beans have been around for a while, they will take longer for the initial cooking. They should be almost tender when you taste; if not, add a little more water and continue to cook until they are to your liking. Beans should not be salted until almost done, so you can remove your dog's portion before the final baking if you are avoiding salt for him.

When they're tender, drain the beans and put them in a small baking dish. Stir in the mushrooms, garlic, lamb chunks, and braising liquid or meat broth. Cover, and bake 20 minutes in a preheated 350-degree oven. Sprinkle parsley all over the top.

# Pasta

Here are a few of my favorite pasta dishes. Make a simple but substantial sauce, often concocted out of some leftovers, while you bring a big pot of salted water to the boil. Then cook the pasta. When the pasta is done *al dente,* toss it together with the sauce and sprinkle on grated cheese. This is a technique I learned from Lidia Bastianich, a master of Italian cooking, that is very useful for the single cook who perhaps gets home late, ready to eat, and with a hungry dog to feed.

# Fusilli with Zucchini, Peppers, and Chicken

Here I use some leftover cooked chicken, but you could substitute some other meat that seems compatible.

Salt
2 tablespoons light olive oil
1 medium zucchini
½ cup sliced mushrooms
3 strips red bell pepper, cut to size similar to the zucchini
3 ounces fusilli

½ cup chicken broth or more as needed
About ¾ cup of shredded cooked chicken
3 scallions, finely sliced
Freshly ground pepper
Grated Parmesan cheese

Set a large pot of water to boil along with a tablespoon each of salt and oil. Sauté the zucchini in the remaining olive oil. After 2 or 3 minutes, add the mushrooms and the bell pepper to the pan, then turn down the heat, cover, and cook slowly. When the water comes to a boil, stir in the pasta. Meanwhile, add the chicken broth, chicken, and scallions to the zucchini and season with salt and pepper to taste. When the pasta is done *al dente*, drain it, reserving a little of the pasta cooking water in case your sauce needs thinning. Scoop up the pasta, and dump it into the zucchini sauce. Warm through, mixing gently. Turn off the heat, correct the seasoning and sauce texture, and add as much cheese as you want.

# Pasta with Liver, Mushrooms, and Cherry Tomatoes

This is a very versatile recipe, as pastas are meant to be. You can use different seasonal vegetables, and you can vary the liver flavor by using some holiday foie gras or pâté that might need eating up, or just a piece of calves' liver. I use soba noodles for a change not just because they taste good with these ingredients, but also because the buckwheat that they are made of is a healthy ingredient.

Salt and freshly ground
    pepper
3 ounces spaghetti or soba
    noodles
1 tablespoon olive oil
1 chicken liver, quartered, and
    a similar amount—or more—
    calves' liver

1 shallot, peeled and finely
    chopped
4 medium sized mushrooms,
    quartered
6 cherry tomatoes, halved
About 3 tablespoons grated
    Parmesan cheese

Set a large pot of salted water to boil. When it is boiling, stir in the spaghetti or soba noodles. Meanwhile, heat 2 teaspoons olive oil in a medium skillet, and quickly sear the liver pieces on both sides. Remove to a small dish, and keep warm. Pour the remaining oil into the skillet, and toss in the shallot, mushrooms, and cherry tomatoes. Sauté quickly, until the vegetables are just tender and the tomatoes have released their liquid. Now return the liver pieces to the pan, and add ⅓ cup of the pasta water, and salt and pepper to taste. When the pasta is done *al dente*, drain, reserving a cup of the pasta water in case you need to thin the sauce. Mix the pasta in with the skillet ingredients, and cook enough to blend flavors, adding more liquid as needed. Turn off the heat, and stir in the grated cheese; I always save a little to top my portion, and Mabon's, too.

# Okra and Bacon Pasta

You wouldn't think okra would be a particularly appealing vegetable to a dog, but when I dressed it up with a bit of bacon, Mabon gobbled it up. The secret is cooking the okra quickly, draining it well, then refreshing it in cold water so it doesn't get gummy, which is what seems to make okra haters squeamish.

5 ounces okra (about 12 pieces)
3 ounces pasta (I prefer penne here)
4 strips bacon, cut into 1-inch lengths
1 tablespoon olive oil
1 fat garlic clove, peeled and slivered

1 large, ripe tomato, peeled, seeded, and diced, or ¾ cup tomato sauce
Salt and freshly ground pepper to taste
Freshly grated Parmesan cheese

Bring a large pot of water to a boil. Drop the okra into the pot, and cook for 3 minutes. Lift the okra out of the water with a large mesh spoon, and dump it into a bowl of chilled water; then drain. Return the okra water to a boil, and stir in the pasta. Meanwhile, cook the bacon until it is brown and cooked through. Dispose of the fat, and remove the bacon to paper towels to drain. Wipe out the skillet and heat the olive oil in it. Cut the okra into 1-inch pieces, and add them to the pan along with the garlic. (I set aside about a third of the okra for Mabon.) Toss the tomato into the pan, and cook rapidly, tossing for a minute or so. When the pasta is done *al dente,* use the mesh spoon to fish out as much as you would like for yourself and your dog, and dump it into the pan. You may need to thin and extend the sauce; if so, add a few tablespoons of the pasta cooking water and season with salt and pepper. Toss in the bacon and as much grated Parmesan as you like.

# Soba Noodles with Smoked Salmon (or Trout) and Spring Asparagus

Soba, the Japanese buckwheat noodles, are nutritious and delicious, particularly when tossed with smoked salmon and spring asparagus. This makes a simple, quick dinner for the two of us.

8-10 asparagus spears, tough ends discarded, the rest cut diagonally into 3 pieces each

3 ounces soba noodles

1 tablespoon light olive oil or vegetable oil

About 6 scallions, including tender green parts, trimmed and cut into 2-inch pieces

6-8 ounces smoked salmon or trout, shredded

Splash of white wine (optional)

Freshly ground pepper

Sprig of fresh basil or cilantro, chopped

1 teaspoon drained and rinsed capers

Bring a large pot of water to a boil, and stir in the asparagus. Boil for 2 minutes, then scoop out the pieces with a strainer and set aside. When the water has returned to a vigorous boil, stir in the soba noodles. Boil about 5–6 minutes. Meanwhile, heat the oil in a small wok or pan, and sauté the scallions for a minute. Add the salmon or trout and a splash of white wine, if using. When the soba are done *al dente,* scoop them up and transfer them to the wok. Toss everything together, adding a little pasta water if needed. Grind some pepper on top and scatter in the herbs and capers. Mabon gave equal attention to all the ingredients here and seemed to down them with relish.

# Vegetables

When Mabon first came to me, he would eat anything his tiny teeth could handle. But now that he is well along in his fourth year, he is more discriminating. If he doesn't like some bitter green that I have tried to mix into his bowl, he will carefully extract the leaves and dump them on the kitchen floor. Sometimes,

*These ready-to-be-roasted vegetables—carrots, parsnips, turnips— look tempting to the young scavenger.*

when he has finished the good stuff, he will return to the little piles of bitter leaves and give them a lick, but usually he walks away from them. So I have to find ways of making what's good for him appealing. Roasting certain vegetables is one way, and it's a challenge that has expanded my own cooking horizons. Roasting can transfer magically a gnarled chunk of celery root or parsnip or turnip into something mellow, almost sweet, and a little chewy.

I try to cook up a whole trayful or two of vegetables, so Mabon can have a variety to draw from during the days ahead. And, I'll admit, I take my fair share when they have just come out of the oven.

Here are guidelines for two trayfuls of vegetables that Mabon and I particularly like. Try them on your pets, and keep a record of their preferences. You may have to adjust timing and oven temperatures in accordance with the season (vegetables picked when they are young are apt to be more tender and cook faster). So be sure to test with a fork and remove pieces from the oven as they are done.

Use a baking sheet (or two), and sprinkle on enough oil to grease them lightly. Spread the vegetables all around, leaving a little space between the pieces so they roast, not steam. Turn them halfway through cooking, and remove when they are done, as indicated in the following lists.

# Tray One

1. *Eggplant.* I shave about a quarter of the skin off, and then cut the eggplant lengthwise into approximately ½- to ¾-inch-thick slices. Brush a little olive oil on both sides, and salt lightly. Roast in a preheated 375-degree oven for 35–40 minutes, turning once. Test after 35 minutes: the flesh should be slightly browned, and soft when you prick it. If you want to soften further, stack the slices and put in a brown paper bag for 10 minutes, or until ready to eat. Try to give your pet slices that don't have seeds.

2. *Carrots.* Peel the carrots, and rub lightly with olive oil. If the carrots are very big, slice at least the thick parts in half lengthwise. Roast in a preheated 375-degree oven for 35–40 minutes.

3. *Zucchini.* Trim ends, and cut the zucchini in half lengthwise. Rub with olive oil, salt lightly, and roast 30 minutes in a preheated 375-degree oven.

4. *Corn.* Leave the husk on, and roast in a preheated 375-degree oven for 35 minutes. When cool enough to handle, pull off leaves and silk, and brush with butter.

5. *Red and/or yellow bell pepper.* Cut the pepper in half lengthwise, remove the ribs and seeds, then cut either in halves or quarters, and roast 35 minutes in a preheated 375-degree oven, skin side up. If you want to peel the pepper pieces, enclose them in a paper bag to steam for 10–15 minutes, then rub off the skin, using a piece of the bag to loosen it and pull it off.

6. *Whole sweet potato.* Roast a whole unpeeled sweet potato or two in a preheated 375-degree oven for 1 hour. After ½ hour of roasting, prick the skin to keep it from bursting. It should be done in 1 hour, or more if very large. Test by pricking deeply into the flesh. It should be very tender.

7. *Fennel.* For roasting, it's important that the fennel is relatively young and plump, not large and stringy. Remove the outer coarse segments and then cut ⅓-inch slices from top to bottom. Rub the slices with olive oil, salt lightly, and roast for about 40 minutes in a 375-degree oven, turning the slices over once.

# Tray Two

1. *Parsnips.* Peel one or two large parsnips, and cut into 2- or 3-inch lengths. The stem end is always much thicker, so split those pieces horizontally. Rub a little oil over, and roast in a preheated 375-degree oven for about 45 minutes, then begin testing. It is done when the fork penetrates quite easily. Remove from the oven.

2. *Celeriac* (or *celery root*). Peeling the ugly celery root is a challenge but worth it. Use a sharp knife to cut off the skin, digging into the flesh to pry out all the dark spots. Cut into slices about 1 inch thick, and paint them with oil. Roast in a preheated 375-degree oven about 50 minutes, then test, and remove from the oven when done.

3. *White turnips.* Tiny early turnips, smaller than golf balls, are a revelation, and no peeling is required—just a little oil rub. For mature turnips, peel and cut them into ¾-inch slices. Both types need about 45 minutes in a preheated 375-degree oven.

4. *Beets.* These fare best if they are foil-wrapped, in which case they take over an hour in a preheated 375-degree oven. Test by inserting a needle into the flesh. When the beets are tender and ready, remove from the oven and let rest in the foil until cool enough to handle, then trim and peel.

5. *Butternut squash.* See page 143 for directions on roasting a butternut-squash "bowl." If you want chunks, cut the peeled squash into ¾-inch pieces.

# Roasted Asparagus

This is adapted from a recipe of Nina Simonds, who introduced me to so many new healthy flavors from the Far East when we worked on her books together. Roasting quickly at a high heat transforms asparagus, and I keep it separate from the other roasting vegetables here because the seasonings are so Asian-accented that I don't want them to mingle. Mabon doesn't care. In fact, this dish has broken down his resistance to asparagus, and I often slip a few spears in with his vegetable quota for dinner now.

¾ pound asparagus
½ teaspoon virgin olive oil

½ teaspoon sesame oil
1 teaspoon toasted sesame seeds

**DRESSING**

1 tablespoon reduced-salt soy sauce

1 teaspoon minced garlic
¾ teaspoon water

Snap off the tough ends of the asparagus spears. Rinse the spears, and drain on paper towels. Spread them out on a large cookie sheet, and toss in the olive oil and sesame oil to coat them. Sprinkle the sesame seeds on top and roast in a preheated 475-degree oven for 4–5 minutes, or until just tender when pierced. Mix the dressing ingredients together, and pour over the asparagus. You and your dog won't eat these all up, but they are delicious cold in a salad or as a garnish for a variety of dishes.

# Corn Cakes

How often several ears of cooked corn left over from a summer corn feast will get thrown out. Not in Mabon's kitchen. I've worked out a recipe that couldn't be simpler and rounds out supper nicely. Or you can make these cakes for breakfast instead: just leave out the herbs in the batter and add a light sprinkling of sugar. And, of course, serve with warm maple syrup.

1 ear of corn, cooked
1 large egg, lightly beaten
2 teaspoons instant flour
2 scallions, including the tender green parts, finely chopped
1 tablespoon chopped fresh
cilantro or parsley (or other herbs to your liking)
Salt and freshly ground pepper to taste
2 tablespoons butter

Using a sharp knife, scrape the corn kernels into a bowl. Remove 1 tablespoon of the egg to a saucer, and mix the rest with the corn kernels, instant flour, scallions, cilantro, and salt and pepper to taste. Form into two cakes—one a third of the size of the other—and coat lightly with the reserved egg, using a pastry brush on both sides. Warm the butter in a small frying pan, and when it starts to sizzle, slip the corn cakes into the pan. Fry over medium to low heat, turning once, until lightly browned. The smaller cake goes to your dog.

You can substitute other vegetables you may have lurking in the fridge (or garden), such as zucchini or carrot or fennel or potatoes—grated or very finely chopped. Experiment, and try this formula to make all kinds of vegetable pancakes, with combinations that your dog seems to like.

*Snoozing again*

# Stir-Fried and Steamed Greens

This is one of the best ways to make your greens taste good, so that your reluctant housemate will at least try spinach, beet greens, Swiss chard, and kale. I know there is a controversy about spinach now—whether it is good for dogs—and the debate over garlic persists. But I feel we should at least try such ingredients, and if they go down well with your dog, you can make them a part of his diet. One reason children developed dislikes of these healthy ingredients was that the greens were cooked so badly, boiled to death, and thereby left an unpleasant smell to linger in the kitchen. So try the greens quickly stir-fried, then steamed, and see if you and your dog don't find them surprisingly good. A wok does the job best, but a largish frying pan will do, too.

About 10 ounces fresh greens—
    spinach, Swiss chard, beet
    greens, or kale
1 tablespoon olive oil

1 garlic clove, peeled and thinly
    sliced
Salt to taste
A few drops of lemon juice

Rinse the greens thoroughly, and cut off any tough stems. Heat the oil in a wok or pan till almost smoking. Throw in the garlic, and brown very lightly. Now dump in the greens with water clinging to them. Stir-fry for a minute. Pour in about ¼ cup water. Cover, and steam-cook rapidly, checking and adding more water as needed to keep the greens moist. Mature greens may take as long as 5 or 6 minutes; very young leaves, only 3 or 4. Check, taste, and finish cooking to your liking (all the water should be absorbed when ready). Salt lightly, and squeeze on a little lemon juice.

# Stuffed Butternut Squash

Too much trouble to stuff a vegetable or two—just for Mabon and me? Not at all. They taste so good and look so appealing that I can't resist. Furthermore, they make good use of whatever tidbits you might have in the fridge, and you can create your own combinations, using this recipe as a guide.

1 round end of a medium-sized butternut squash
½ cup cooked brown rice (see page 102)
Pinch of dried tarragon or sage
Salt and freshly ground pepper to taste

⅓ cup finely chopped cooked meat (ham and prosciutto are particularly good)
A sprinkling of olive oil
About 2 tablespoons fresh breadcrumbs
1 tablespoon aged grating cheese

Roast the round bottom of the butternut squash in a preheated 400-degree oven for about 40 minutes, then start testing by piercing it with a fork to see if it is tender. If not, roast longer; the time will vary considerably, depending on the age and size of the squash. When it is almost soft, remove the squash from the oven. While it cools, mix the brown rice, seasonings, and meat together. Now scrape out the meaty interior of the squash, leaving a standup border all around; mix in with the stuffing. Fill the squash with this stuffing, sprinkle a little olive oil over all, and top with the breadcrumbs and cheese. Bake in a preheated 350-degree oven for 30 minutes.

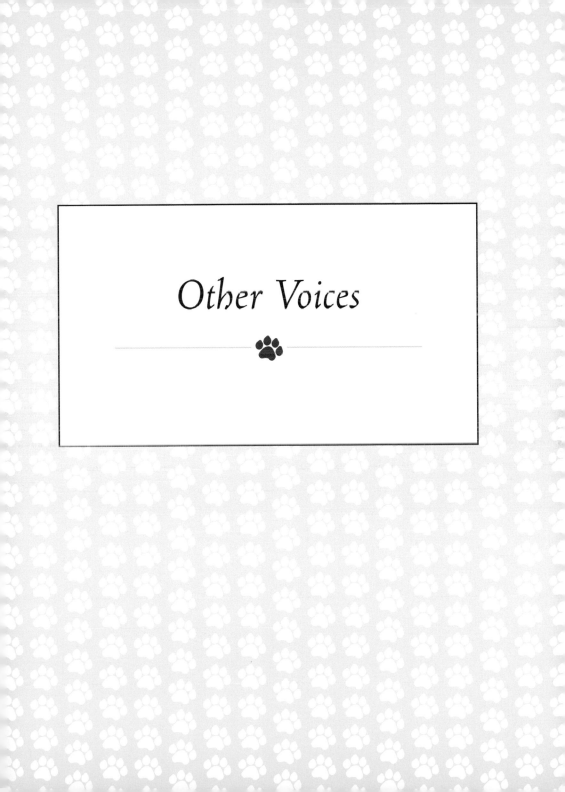

# Other Voices

I find that when I ask fellow dog lovers what they feed to their pets, I am often met with a guilty look, and they admit to using canned and dried foods. Then they add: "But I include some vegetables and maybe some leftover meat so it's not all the commercial stuff. . . . Is that okay?" In other words, they feel guilty about giving the creatures they care for something that isn't commercially produced. So I asked some friends and colleagues to speak up and tell of their experiences, and also to offer some useful suggestions.

When I talked to Jacques Pépin, who has what he calls a "big miniature poodle," he told me about a pellet called "Royal Canin" that is made exclusively for poodles, that royal breed. He has found it a useful addition to his dog's dinner, but by no means a replacement for the vegetables—carrots, peas, string beans, etc.—and for whatever dish the Pépins may be having for their own dinner. His dog loves cheese, so why shouldn't he get a taste for breakfast, and maybe for supper, too? In other words, this dog is a member of Jacques's family—lucky fellow.

Recently I talked with Vicky Wilson, my friend and colleague at Knopf, who pointed out that it isn't always so easy to switch to a home-cooked diet if your dog has been raised on commercial fare. The sudden change can bring on a severe and often persistent case of diarrhea. So go slowly.

Vicky's household today consists of two dogs and three cats, and they thrive on two meals a day made up of a good brand of commercial food, some fresh vegetables, and a teaspoon of cottage cheese on top. Vicky believes in having several pets around so that they can play together and enjoy long walks of at least a mile every day with a walker they know well.

The other voices in this section are from animal lovers who have also created healthy, happy homes for animals they love.

*Julia always welcomed household pets but it was too difficult with her way of life to have a cat or a dog living with her year-round. So instead friends and neighbors would often provide a guest companion. She urged me to bring Madoc whenever I visited her in Cambridge. Here she is visiting us in Vermont.*

M. F. K. Fisher: *"I would never give a dog or cat something I would not eat myself."*

# A Wonderful Thing

Lisa Whitney, D.V.M.

I still do think home cooking is a wonderful thing to do for your pets. It allows you to control the quality of the food you put into their bodies and eliminates the aspect of food processing that commercial dog food, by definition, depends upon. For those who find organic, local, or sustainable food important, it is an opportunity to embrace that for your pet as well. They say you are what you eat, and there is probably more truth to that than we know. I don't think food gets enough credit for maintaining and creating health. I think we will continue to find that much of our health and illness, as well as that of our pets, is determined by the quality of the nutrition we provide. It is such an easy thing to take control of what goes into our pets' bodies. Even those of us who don't have time to cook full-time for our pets can supplement commercial foods with whole foods, and then feel good that we have improved upon our pets' diet.

Freeze-dried foods can be a nice option, especially for those who want less-processed food without spending the added time to cook for their pets. I don't personally feel raw food is a bad thing (although this is a HUGE can of worms, and you will find individuals who have VERY strong feelings about the issue one way or the other). I do think that one needs to be very careful about feeding pets raw food, because of the potential risk of bacterial contamination to both pets and humans. *E. coli* and salmonella rarely cause clinical symptoms in

domestic animals, but they certainly can in people. There is a risk in handling the raw foods, as well as the pets' fecal material.

"Natural" is a marketing ploy and means nothing. Almost all of my clients, when asked what they feed their dogs, answer something about "natural." It is very en vogue right now, as are "grain-free" foods (which may make some sense for cats, but are meaningless for dogs, who can eat grains without any trouble). Which comes back around to one of the main things I like about home cooking: you know what is going into the food and where it comes from. If "natural" is important, you can determine what that means to you and seek it out. A great diet can help make a wonderfully healthy pet. But an inadequate diet can just as easily lead to health problems.

# It Takes Only Five Minutes!

Haidi Kuhn Segal

From childhood on, I lived with animals: dogs, cats, and horses. In my family, it was taken for granted that the animals were part of our life; accordingly, they got good and understanding care.

I was born in Estonia before World War II and grew up in Germany, Poland, Czechoslovakia, Luxembourg, and Belgium. In those days, canned food and biscuits for dogs and cats did not exist, so my mother cooked for our animals. I never thought there was another way, and our dogs and cats were healthy and lived long lives.

By the time I started dividing my time between the United States and Europe in the 1960s, always with my pets in tow, it seemed only natural, given my background, to cook for my dogs, mostly longhaired dachshunds, cocker spaniels, and medium-sized abandoned mutts. It is easily done, does not take much time, and is less expensive than buying industrially produced foods. Also, I know what is *in* the homemade meals I serve my animals.

Usually, in one small pot I boil meat (veal heart if I can find it, chicken, turkey, or reasonably priced beef) in water for five to ten minutes, depending on the size of the meat chunks, so I obtain a rich broth. I try to leave the beef slightly pink inside. In a second small pot I boil rice and/or oatmeal and cut-up fresh vegetables (string beans, carrots, broccoli, parsley, and others). Then, when the pots are cool, they go into the refrigerator; their contents will make meals for two to three days.

(I cook the rice, as usual, in plain water, together with the vegetables. I cook the oatmeal only for a short while and then let it soak and swell for about six minutes.)

To serve the daily meal to our dog, I take both pots out of the refrigerator. Often there will be a layer of congealed fat on top of the cold meat broth. I just lift it off with a knife or spoon and throw it away. I cut the cold meat into bite-sized pieces, and I warm up some of the broth. Then I put the cold oatmeal/rice/vegetable mixture into the dog's usual bowl and mix it with the warmed-up meat broth and the cold pieces of meat. That's it. Once you have prepared these basics, it takes only five minutes to put your dog's meal together. And both pots go back into the refrigerator to be used for future meals.

Sometimes I put grated raw carrots into this lukewarm meal, but I never add salt or pepper to the dog's food. I feed white meat to aging dogs; it's better for them than red meat, according to all the vets I've asked.

My last three dogs lived to be eighteen.

# They Eat Better Than I Do?
# That's Okay with Me

Bobbie Bristol

When we got our first dog, Willie (a poodle/Lab mix), it was impressed upon me that his mother only ate the BARF diet (Bones and Raw Food) and that I should give him the same. For about a year, I dutifully bought chicken legs and whacked them into bite-sized pieces and added a little flaxseed oil and a little nutritional yeast. But I found it worrisome that Willie sometimes gagged and coughed up little bits of bone. So, by the time we got a second dog, Maggie (a black poodle/golden retriever mix), I decided that I was going to cook all the chicken and take it off the bone.

By process of elimination, I found that chicken thighs were the easiest chicken parts to debone. There are no little pointy bonelike things hiding anywhere; you don't have to worry that a sharp rib has sneaked into the dog bowl. All you have is one obvious, uncomplicated thigh bone. I buy the thighs in family packs—they are often on sale. They are labeled as coming from young chickens not raised on antibiotics. I throw them into a stew pot about once a week with a lot of water, and cook them until they are almost falling off the bone. When I find a bulk package of hearts and gizzards, I add them to the stew. If I were smart and efficient, I would debone all the thighs at once, when they are cool (instead of in nightly installments), so let's say that's what I do.

I degrease the chicken broth, usually saving some for my own uses but most of it is for the dogs. To the big bowl of chicken meat I add five or six baked sweet potatoes, peeled and chopped up, and either cooked rice or oatmeal. Then I add back a good bit of the chicken broth, so the mush is good and wet. The dogs eat this happily most nights. I came up with this combination by looking at the ingredients in a good bag of dry dog food and found that sweet potato, rice, and oatmeal were always mentioned.

I vary this diet once a week or so with sautéed chicken livers, beef liver, or beef heart (which I either stew or sauté). I also add cooked green vegetables when I have them—broccoli, kale, green beans. My dogs also like sardines quite a bit.

I am aware that one of the virtues of the raw diet is that dogs get to eat raw bones and all the excellent things found in bone marrow, and my dogs don't get that except when I buy them a beef bone to gnaw on. So I hedge my bets: In the morning, Willie and Maggie get a very good dry dog food for breakfast, which has a goodly supply of vitamins, minerals, and calcium in it. They like it fine, but they eat it in a leisurely fashion throughout the day. The chicken dinner is devoured very quickly.

To give you a rough idea of how much I feed these sixty- to seventy-pound pups, every day each gets at least one chicken thigh (or three split between them), half a sweet potato, a good dollop of oatmeal or rice, and a cup or so of chicken broth.

Willie, because he is three-quarters poodle, has a poodle's fastidious taste. He approaches any dog bowl placed in front of him with studied indifference, sniffs at it, looks away, sighs, and then slowly begins to eat. Maggie's dominant nature is golden retriever. She is a masterful food thief (but that's a whole other tale). She has her nose in her bowl even before I have put it on the floor, and proceeds to inhale her dinner. When she has licked her bowl clean, she walks over to Willie's bowl

*Willie and Maggie awaiting their supper*

and fixes him with an intense look while he continues, now somewhat self-consciously, to eat most of his dinner. Eventually, he sighs again and walks away, generously leaving a couple of scraps of sweet potato for Maggie to polish off.

All of this is pretty simple and straightforward, especially if you bone and mix the ingredients all at once. There are times during the week when I know that the dogs are eating better than I am. And that's okay with me.

*David Nussbaum with his pal Madoc*

# Good Boy (or Girl) Biscotti

David Nussbaum

I first came to know Judith when we were working together in Cambridge, Massachusetts, on Julia Child's last book, the companion volume to the delightful TV series *Julia and Jacques Cooking at Home*. While Julia and Jacques were sparring with each other and improvising new recipes in the kitchen below, Judith and I were on the landing above, trying to take down the recipe details from a monitor and hushing Judith's dog Madoc, whom she had brought with her from New York. Madoc and I became immediate pals, and I would take him for walks around the streets of Cambridge to escape from the huge television production taking place in Julia's kitchen. Madoc was panicky about people, and his acceptance of me made Judith happy and fostered our long friendship, as is often the case when one "dog person" meets another.

What did not make Judith so happy, though, was my immoderation in greeting Madoc with treats from my pocket and tidbits from our many recipe tests. You'll spoil him, she said. But handing out a morsel with crunch and flavor—for no good reason other than the pleasure it gave both receiver and giver—was what I did with all my own hounds and mutts. Madoc was a great guy, and every treat, we both knew, showed that I loved him.

These days, I live on a small farmstead with an ever-increasing number of residents—poultry, equines, canine, and feline—and I'm reminded every day by clucks, neighs, brays, barks, and meows that every animal loves treats. And, like Madoc, all learn quickly that I'm an easy touch. Fortunately, all (except the cat) love bread, which in various forms is in unending supply in my kitchen. I regularly bake mixed-grain sourdough bread and buttermilk biscuits; I buy bagels, bialys, baguettes, ciabattas, and sandwich loaves.

Of course, it doesn't all get eaten by me. The crusts and crumbs from my store of breadstuffs become the daily delights of my menagerie. There's a cookie jar of dried bread chunks and bagel chips for the horses and donkey in the barn, and one on the kitchen counter for the dog. Morning and night, I take a couple of slices of still-soft bread out to the henhouse and tear and scatter the bits in their yard, setting off a stampede of cackling and pecking.

On occasion, though, especially in winter, when there's time and a hot oven helps warm the farmhouse, I make a big yeast bread round with oatmeal, vegetables, fats, and sweetening, just for the animals. The interior crumb is moist and dense; a good portion of that gets torn and crumbled for the birds. But most of the loaf, including all of the crust, gets sliced into bite-sized pieces and baked a second time—hence *biscotti*—to achieve the hardness preferred by discriminating dogs and equines.

What follows is a rough proportional guide for Good Boy (or Girl) *Biscotti*. The basics of mine are oatmeal, whole-wheat flour, and carrots; you can vary the ingredients and amounts with whatever's on hand and to your pal's taste.

For a big loaf (to bake in a 3–4-quart casserole), stir together about 3 cups rolled oats with 5 cups wheat flour, a teaspoon or two of salt, and a scant teaspoon of granulated yeast (the kind that doesn't require proofing). Grate carrots—or carrots and butternut squash—to get 3 cups of shreds, and toss them in.

Measure and stir together all the liquid ingredients to total about 3 cups, starting with ⅓ to ½ cup each of vegetable oil and molasses. Got extra eggs? Beat in 2 to 4. Milk? Apple juice? Use it up. Water will make up the balance.

Pour all the wet stuff into the dry stuff—or vice versa—and stir purposefully. What you want is a dough that's stiff and uniformly moistened, even if sticky. Scrape the bowl to bring the dough into a mass: it should hold its shape. If it's too wet, add wheat flour; too dry, stir in liquid.

Oil the casserole, and turn the dough into it. Cover or seal with plastic wrap, and let it alone for 10–12 hours. It should have risen perceptibly by then; if it threatens to overflow, knock it back.

Bake in a preheated 375-degree oven for an hour, or until it's firm to the touch. Let the dough cool, in the casserole or out, then slice it into the size and thickness you want. Array *biscotti* on a baking sheet, and dry them in a low oven until they're too hard for a human jaw to crunch without incurring major dental work.

*Mabon with my son, Chris, the photographer*

# Acknowledgments

Thanks, of course, to Mabon, the inspiration for this book. And to my son, Chris, whose camera caught the spirit of Mabon's life in both Vermont and the Big City. Chris's help in getting the book started was a great blessing. Then Evelyn McNichol of Shelburne, Vermont, pitched in, and finally Sean Picone and Meghan Houser of Knopf editorial used their skills at the computer to bring the text together.

It was particularly rewarding working again with the Knopf team of Maria Massey, who shepherded the book into production; designer Kristen Bearse, who always comes up with delightfully creative ideas; and Carol Devine Carson, for the endearing jacket. I am grateful to all of you.

I am particularly indebted to my fellow dog-loving editor Jonathan Segal for his encouraging help and to Sonny Mehta, who believed in the idea from the start.

Finally, I am enormously grateful to Dr. Lisa Whitney, Haidi Kuhn Segal, Bobbie Bristol, and David Nussbaum for sharing the pleasures they have with their animal companions.

# Index

(Page references in *italic* refer to illustrations.)

Bristol, Bobbie, 155–57
broccoli, 9
  Chicken Pieces with Seasonal
    Vegetables, *64*, 64–65
  Grits with Shrimp, 108–9
  Stir-Fry of Chicken and Seasonal
    Vegetables, 66–67
Broccoli Rabe, Roast Beef Shoulder
  with, 32–33
broiled:
  Chicken Legs and Thighs, 62
  Haddock, Bluefish, or Mackerel
    over a Bed of Fennel and
    Potatoes, 92
  Salmon, 96
brown rice, 101
  Brown Rice (recipe), 102
  A Casserole of Rice and Vegetables,
    103
  Stuffed Butternut Squash, 143
Brussels Sprouts, A Steamed Egg
  Nestled in, 81
Bryn Teg (Vermont home), 20–22
buckwheat:
  Kasha, 118
  *see also* soba noodles
Burgers, Turkey, 76, *77*
butternut squash:
  Chicken Breast with Winter Squash,
    Fennel, and Hazelnuts, 70
  in David Nussbaum's Good Boy (or
    Girl) *Biscotti*, 160–63, *161*, *162*
  roasting, 138
  Stuffed, 143

**C**

calves' liver:
  and Bacon, 46

Pasta with Mushrooms, Cherry
  Tomatoes and, 127
carrot(s):
  Braised Beef Shanks, 34–35
  Cakes, 140
  in David Nussbaum's Good Boy (or
    Girl) *Biscotti*, 160–63, *161*, *162*
  roasting, 135
  Stir-Fry of Pork, Seasonal
    Vegetables, and Almonds,
    48–50, *49*
casseroles:
  Chicken and Asparagus Gratin, 72
  Moussaka, 58–59
  Pork and Leek au Gratin, 51
  of Rice and Vegetables, 103
  Shepherd's Beef or Lamb Pie,
    44–45
Catfish Fillet, Panfried, 94
celeriac (or celery root), roasting, 134,
  138
Central Park (New York City), letting
  dogs off the leash in, 25–26
cheese(s), 147
  A Frittata, 89
  as omelet filling, 84
  semi-soft, in A Steamed Egg Nestled
    in Brussels Sprouts, 81
chicken:
  and Asparagus Gratin, 72
  Breast with Winter Squash, Fennel,
    and Hazelnuts, 70
  Fusilli with Zucchini, Peppers, and,
    126
  heart and gizzard, 60, 80
  leftover, as omelet filling, 84
  Legs and Thighs, Grilled or
    Broiled, 62

prosciutto:
  Baked Polenta, 113
  as omelet filling, 84
  Stuffed Butternut Squash, 143
protein foods, *see* beef; chicken; eggs;
    fish; lamb; meat; pork; poultry
Pyramide, La (near Vienne, France),
    23–24

Q
quinoa, 11
  Lemon-Flavored, with Vegetables,
    114–15

R
raw diet for dogs, 151–52, 155, 156
Red Lentils, 120
Reynolds, John, 88
rice, 101–7
  brown, 101
  Brown (recipe), 102
  brown, in Stuffed Butternut Squash,
    143
  A Casserole of Vegetables and, 103
  chicken, and sweet potato mush,
    Bobbie Bristol's, 155–57
  meat, oatmeal, and vegetable
    mixture, Haidi Kuhn Segal's,
    153–54
  varieties of, 101
  Wild Mushroom Risotto, 107
  *see also* wild rice
Risotto, Wild Mushroom, 107
roast(ed):
  Asparagus, 139
  Beef Shoulder with Broccoli Rabe,
    32–33
  Cornish Game Hen, 73

trayfuls of vegetables, 134–38
  Whole Fish, 91
Royal Canin, 147

S
Salad, Chicken, Noodle, and
    Vegetable, 68–69
Sally MacGregor (Scottie), 6, 13–16,
    *14, 15*
salmon:
  Broiled or Grilled, 96
  Cakes, 97
  as omelet filling, 84
  skin, too fatty for dogs, 96
  Smoked, Soba Noodles with Spring
    Asparagus and, 129
sardines, 19, 90
Sauce, Cream, or Béchamel, 43
sausage:
  Frittata, 89
  Green Lentils with Mushrooms and,
    119
  as omelet filling, 84
scallions, in Wild Rice Pilaf, 105
Scrap Soup, 37
seafood:
  Grits with Shrimp, 108–9
  *see also* fish
seasonings, removing pet's portion
    before adding to your own, 9–10,
    50, 120
Segal, Haidi Kuhn, 153–54
Shepherd's Beef or Lamb Pie,
    44–45
Shirred Egg, 80
Shrimp, Grits with, 108–9
Simonds, Nina, 139
smell, dog's sense of, 86–88

## A Note About the Author

Judith Jones joined Alfred A. Knopf in 1957, and she officially retired in 2011. The writers she edited include John Updike, Anne Tyler, William Maxwell, and John Hersey. And the cookbook authors she edited include Julia Child, Lidia Bastianich, James Beard, Marion Cunningham, Rosie Daley, Marcella Hazan, Madhur Jaffrey, Edna Lewis, Joan Nathan, Jacques Pépin, Claudia Roden, and Nina Simonds. She is the author of *The Tenth Muse: My Life in Food* and *The Pleasures of Cooking for One.* She is also the coauthor with Evan Jones (her late husband) of *The Book of Bread; Knead It, Punch It, Bake It!* (for children); and *The Book of New New England Cookery,* and collaborated with Angus Cameron on *The L.L. Bean Game and Fish Cookbook.* Recently, she has contributed to *Vogue* and *Savour.* In 2006, she was awarded the James Beard Foundation Lifetime Achievement Award.